Welcome to the
BEAR
Handbook!

Contents

                                                                    Pages
Parent Guide..1–8
Welcome to the Bear Trail 9
How Baloo Taught Mowgli the Law of the Pack...................9

Bobcat Trail........................12–23

1. Cub Scout Promise 13
2. The Law of the Pack 15
3 Meaning of Webelos...16
4 Cub Scout Sign...17
5. Cub Scout Handshake.......................................18
6. Cub Scout Motto 19
7. Cub Scout Salute 20
8. Child Protection Exercises................................21
Bobcat Trail Record...22
Your Den, Pack, and Uniform.................................23

Bear Trail (Achievements) 24–117

1. Ways We Worship 26
2. Emblems of Faith...30
3. What Makes America Special? 34

Illustrations of Baloo by Robert Depew

33451
ISBN 0-8395-3451-5
© 2003 Boy Scouts of America
2008 Printing

4. Tall Tales 42
5 Sharing Your World with Wildlife 50
6. Take Care of Your Planet 56
7. Law Enforcement Is a Big Job 64
8. The Past Is Exciting and Important 72
9. What's Cooking? 80
10. Family Fun 90
11. Be Ready 96
12. Family Outdoor Adventures 106
13. Saving Well, Spending Well 112
14. Ride Right 118
15. Games, Games, Games! 126
16. Building Muscles 130
17. Information, Please 136
18. Jot It Down 140
19. Shavings and Chips 146
20. Sawdust and Nails 152
21. Build a Model 156
22. Tying It All Up 162
23. Sports, Sports, Sports! 170
24. Be a Leader 174

Arrow Point Trail (Electives) 180–278

1. Space 182
2. Weather 184
3. Radio 190
4. Electricity 192
5. Boats 196
6. Aircraft 202
7. Things That Go 206
8. Cub Scout Band 210
9. Art 214
10. Masks 218
11. Photography 222
12. Nature Crafts 226
13. Magic 230
14. Landscaping 236
15. Water and Soil Conservation 240
16. Farm Animals 244
17. Repairs 246
18. Backyard Gym 250
19. Swimming 254

20. Sports. 260
21. Sales. 266
22. Collecting Things 268
23. Maps. 270
24. American Indian Life. 272
25. Let's Go Camping! 276

Getting Set to be a Webelos Scout 279
How to Wear Cub Scout Insignia. 281
Cub Scout World Conservation Award. 282
Cub Scout Leave No Trace Awareness Award. 283
Cub Scout Outdoor Activity Award. 284
Cub Scout Academics and Sports 286
Bear Trail Record. 288
Arrow Point Trail Record 290

How to help your son follow the Bobcat, Bear, and Arrow Point trails

If you could give your son the greatest gift of all, what would it be? It wouldn't be money or anything money can buy. Whether you are rich or poor, the greatest gift is within your power because that gift is helping a boy become a person with a good feeling about himself and a genuine concern for others. Cub Scouting can help you provide this gift.

Your Son, Cub Scouting, and You

As a parent or guardian, you want your son to grow up to be self-reliant and dependable—a person of worth, a caring individual. Scouting has these same goals in mind for him.

Since 1910 we've been weaving lifetime values into fun and educational activities designed to help parents teach their sons how to make good decisions throughout their lives and give them confidence as they become the adult leaders of tomorrow.

In a society where your son is often taught that winning is every-thing, Cub Scouting teaches him to *do his best* and *be helpful to others* as expressed in the Cub Scout Promise, motto, and Law of the Pack.

The Bear den will involve your son in a group of boys his own age where he can earn status and recognition. There he will also gain a sense of personal achievement from the new skills he learns.

The Purposes of Cub Scouting

Cub Scouting is a year-round family-oriented part of the BSA program designed for boys who are in first through fifth grades (or are 7, 8, 9, and 10 years old). Parents, leaders, and organizations work together to achieve the 10 purposes of Cub Scouting:

1. Character Development
2. Spiritual Growth
3. Good Citizenship
4. Sportsmanship and Fitness
5. Family Understanding
6. Respectful Relationships
7. Personal Achievement
8. Friendly Service
9. Fun and Adventure
10. Preparation for Boy Scouts

Cub Scouting

Your Cub Scout is a member of a Bear Cub Scout den. Most dens have six to eight boys in them and meet once a week. Den meetings are a time for learning new things and having fun. Dens are led by a team of adult volunteers—the den leader and assistant den leader(s). Den leaders are usually adult family members of boys in the den.

Your Cub Scout is also a member of a pack. Packs consist of several dens. Most packs meet once a month. Pack meetings usually follow a suggested theme and are a time for boys to be recognized for their accomplishments during the month, to perform skits and songs they've learned in den meetings, and to have fun with the entire family.

Packs are led by a Cubmaster and pack committee. Like the den leaders, the Cubmaster and assistants are volunteers and are usually adult family members of boys in the pack. Most pack committees consist of adult family members and members of the pack's chartered organization. The pack committee makes plans for pack meetings and activities and takes care of the "business" items necessary for a quality pack program.

The pack is owned by a community organization that is granted a charter by the Boy Scouts of America to use the Scouting program. This chartered organization might be a school, service club, religious group, or other group interested in youth. The chartered organization approves the leadership of the pack, provides a meeting place, and operates the pack within the guidelines and policies of the organization and the Boy Scouts of America.

Akela's OK

As you look through this book, you'll see places for "Akela's OK." That usually means your okay. Akela (ah-KAY-la) is the boy's leader. At home, that is you; at den meetings, it is the den leader; at school, it is the teacher. Almost all electives and achievements are done by you and your Cub Scout at home, not in the den meeting. This book is filled with more than 200 pages of activities for you and your son to enjoy together. Once your Cub Scout has done his best, you can approve the completion of the requirement and the den leader will record his progress in the den records.

David Gilbreath   [date here]   *Karen Bass*

Akela's OK for the Bear trail   Date   Recorded by the den leader

Notes for Akela

Throughout the *Bear Handbook*, special notes for you are printed along with the requirements for special projects that require the supervision and participation of adults. Watch for these "Notes for Akela." They are printed in a smaller, different typestyle for your easy identification. This is an example:

> NOTE for Akela: This is a note for the parent, guardian, or other adult helping a Bear Cub Scout along the trail.

Character Connections

Cub Scouting's Character Connections program helps your son *know, commit,* and *practice* Cub Scouting's 12 core values while enjoying fun and adventure in his Webelos den. This symbol identifies Character Connections throughout this book and in other Cub Scouting materials.

Cub Scouting's 12 Core Values

1. **Citizenship:** Contributing service and showing responsibility to local, state, and national communities.

2. **Compassion:** Being kind and considerate, and showing concern for the well-being of others.

3. **Cooperation:** Being helpful and working together with others toward a common goal.

4. **Courage:** Being brave and doing what is right regardless of our fears, the difficulties, or the consequences.

5. **Faith:** Having inner strength and confidence based on our trust in God.

6. **Health and Fitness:** Being personally committed to keeping our minds and bodies clean and fit.

7. **Honesty:** Telling the truth and being worthy of trust.

8. **Perseverance:** Sticking with something and not giving up, even if it is difficult.

9. **Positive Attitude:** Being cheerful and setting our minds to look for and find the best in all situations.

10. **Resourcefulness:** Using human and other resources to their fullest.

11. **Respect:** Showing regard for the worth of something or someone.

12. **Responsibility:** Fulfilling our duty to God, country, other people, and ourselves.

The Bobcat Trail

In Rudyard Kipling's story, *The Jungle Book*, the black panther Bagheera is the mighty hunter who teaches the cubs the skills of the jungle. In Cub Scouting we use the symbol of the Bobcat. The Bobcat rank is for all boys who join Cub Scouting. If your boy joined Cub Scouting as a Bear Cub Scout, he must earn the Bobcat badge before receiving any other award or rank. You'll find his trail (the requirements) on pages 12 through 23.

Along this trail are the Cub Scout Promise, the Law of the Pack, and the Cub Scout motto. These are the three most important things a boy must learn because they will help him through all of the trails of Scouting.

One part of the Bobcat trail is to read and complete the exercises in the booklet *How to Protect Your Children from Child Abuse*. Child abuse is a problem in our society, and this booklet will help you help your child to avoid potentially abusive situations. **Note:** The booklet is provided as a a tear-out section in the front of this book. Please do tear it out (that makes the book easier to handle), read it carefully, and keep it for easy reference.

When you and your son have followed the eight tracks of the Bobcat, your son may wear his Bobcat badge. It will be presented at the pack meeting.

The Bear Trail

After your Cub Scout has earned his Bobcat badge, he can start along the Bear trail. This is a big adventure for a boy, one the Boy Scouts of America hopes all boys will complete. The Bobcat trail has only eight tracks; the Bear trail is much longer. The Bear trail has 24 achievements, 12 of which a boy must complete to earn the Bear badge.

Once you have okayed the proper achievements, he will have achieved the rank of Bear Cub Scout. How quickly your boy progresses is up to him—and you. He should do his best to complete each achievement. That's part of the promise he made to become a Bobcat, and it is the Cub Scout motto—Do Your Best. Don't okay an achievement if you both know that he can do a better job. Go on to something else, and then go back and try again.

The important thing is to keep him interested by working on the trail with him as often as possible.

Progress Toward Ranks

Your son doesn't have to wait until he completes his entire Bear trail before being recognized for his work. When he completes any three achievements that are required for the Bear rank, his den leader can present the Progress Toward Ranks emblem to him (or if he was a Wolf, he can add to his current emblem). It's a diamond-shaped emblem with a plastic thong attached, and it's worn on the right pocket button of his uniform shirt. Each time he completes three achievements on the Bear trail, he will receive a red bead. After he gets his fourth red bead, he will be ready to receive his Bear badge at a pack meeting.

The Arrow Point Trail

Your Cub Scout can also search the Arrow Point trail. On the Bear trail, the main sections were called achievements, things that we would like all boys to do. On the Arrow Point trail, the main sections are called electives, choices that a boy can make on his own and with your guidance. Achievements that were not used to earn the Bear badge may be used as electives. However, note that unused parts of achievements that were used for the Bear badge may **not** be counted toward Arrow Points.

When your Bear Cub Scout has completed his first ten electives, he will be eligible for a Gold Arrow Point. For every ten additional electives he completes, the Bear Cub Scout qualifies for a Silver Arrow Point to wear beneath the Gold. He can earn as many Silver Arrow Points as he wants until he completes the third grade (or turns 10). Arrow Points are presented at a pack meeting after he receives his Bear badge. Although a boy may work on his Bear Arrow Points at any time after joining the Bear den, they will not be presented until after he receives his Bear badge.

Because some Arrow Point electives may be earned more than once (in different ways), the place for signing "Akela's OK" is different than it is for the Bear trail. Here is an example:

No.	Date	Akela's OK	✓ Den Chart
23.			
23.			
23.			
23.			
23.			

When your Cub Scout completes an elective requirement, enter the letter for that requirement and the date he completed it, and add your signature for Akela's OK. When the den leader has recorded it, check it off under "Den Chart."

Your Cub Scout can keep track of the achievement and elective requirements he has earned on pages 288–290.

Do Your Best

When has a boy completed an elective or achievement? When he, in your opinion as Akela, has completed the skill to the best of his ability. In Cub Scouting, boys are judged against their own standard, not against other boys.

If your Cub Scout has a mental or physical disability that prevents him from attempting an achievement, talk to your Cubmaster about using an elective as an alternative.

The Boy Scouts of America hereby authorizes you, who have read this Parent Guide, to act as Akela. Indicate your willingness to serve by signing below.

I/We will be Akela in this *Bear Handbook*:

Signature _____ Date _____

Signature _____ Date _____

Signature _____ Date _____

Welcome to the Bear Trail!

Read the next few pages in your new *Bear Handbook*. Find out how Baloo helped Mowgli learn the Law of the Pack.

How Baloo Taught Mowgli the Law of the Pack

Long ago in the jungles of India a small boy was separated from his family when his village was raided by the fierce tiger Shere Kahn. He was found and protected by a family of wolves who lived in the jungle. They named him Mowgli and asked Akela, the leader, if he could join their pack. The pack council met once a month at full moon. Akela asked, "Who speaks for this cub?" At first there was no answer, but then Baloo, the wise old brown bear who taught the wolf cubs the Law of the Pack, stood up on his hind paws and said, "I speak for the man-cub. I will teach him."

Bagheera, the black panther, slipped into the council ring and said, "I, too, speak for the man-cub." Shere Kahn snarled in rage. This is how Mowgli came to live with the wolf family in the jungle and learned the ways of a wolf cub.

As Mowgli grew older, Baloo taught him the Law of the Pack and the secret master words that let him talk to the other jungle creatures—all except the Bandar-log, the monkey people who did not obey the Law of the Pack. They had decided to make their own law and thought it would be a fine idea to capture Mowgli and make him their leader. They were so thoughtless and silly the other animals paid no attention to them.

The Bandar-log grabbed Mowgli one day while he was taking a nap. They carried him high above the trees to a deserted village where none of the other jungle creatures lived. While he was being carried through the branches, Mowgli called for help. Chil, the kite (hawk), heard him call and flew swiftly to tell Baloo and Bagheera.

Baloo and Bagheera were furious. They could not follow through the treetops, but they set out on foot through the jungle to rescue Mowgli. Baloo knew that the Bandar-log's greatest fear was of Kaa, the 30-foot-long python. "He can climb as well as they can. Let us go to Kaa," Baloo said.

"What can he do?" asked Bagheera. "He is not of our tribe, and he has the most evil eyes."

"He is old and cunning. Above all, he is always hungry," said Baloo hopefully.

Kaa agreed to help, and the three set off to find Mowgli. They reached the village at nightfall. Bagheera and Baloo moved in first. The Bandar-log swarmed over them, biting and scratching, for the monkey people are brave only when the odds are in their favor. Things were going badly for Baloo and Bagheera when Kaa appeared. Baloo was right; the Bandar-log were terribly frightened of Kaa. Some of them climbed the walls and towers of the city, trying to get as far away as possible; some froze in terror. Kaa battered through the wall of the ancient building where Mowgli was being held captive and set him free.

Kaa began weaving in his hunger dance, making all who watched—the Bandar-log, Baloo, and Bagheera—helpless to move. Mowgli shook his friends who were falling under Kaa's spell and woke them just in time. The three made their escape back to their own part of the jungle.

Mowgli had learned to live as a wolf cub and had begun to learn the wisdom of the bear, but he needed older friends to teach him things that would protect him. Like Mowgli, you can call on parents and leaders to help you.

Bobcat Trail

Welcome to Our Pack!

Say hi to my friend the Bobcat. He has eight things for you to do.

HE SAYS

"Follow my Bobcat Trail."

Fill in this track when you have completed all the Bobcat tracks. You may also mark the Trail Record on page 22. When you have filled in all eight tracks, you can wear the Bobcat badge.

Cub Scout Promise

I, ... ,

promise to do my best
To do my duty to God and
my country,
To help other people, and
To obey the Law of the Pack.

When you say you will do something, that is a *promise.*

Duty to God means:
Put God first. Do what you know God wants you to do.

And my country means:
Do what you can for your country. Be proud that you are an American.

To help other people means:
Do things for others that would help them.

Obey the Law of the Pack means:
Do what Akela asks you to do. Be a good Cub Scout. Be proud that you are one.

Honesty

Know. Discuss these questions with your family: What is a promise? What does it mean to "keep your word?" What does *honesty* mean? What does it mean to "do your best?"

Commit. Discuss these questions with your family. Why is a promise important? Why is it important for people to trust you when you give your word? When might it be difficult to keep your word? List examples.

Practice. Discuss with family members why it is important to be trustworthy and honest and how you can do your best to be honest when you are doing the activities in Cub Scouting.

When you can say the Cub Scout Promise and have completed the Honesty Character Connection, fill in my track.

Akela's OK _____ Date _____ Recorded by the den leader

Say the Law of the Pack. Tell what it means.

The Cub Scout follows Akela (say Ah-KAY-la).
- Akela is a good leader.
- Your mother or father or other adult member of your family is Akela.
- In the pack, your Cubmaster is Akela.
- Your den leader is Akela.
- At school, your teacher is Akela.

The Law of the Pack

The Cub Scout follows Akela.
The Cub Scout helps the pack go.
The pack helps the Cub Scout grow.
The Cub Scout gives goodwill.

The Cub Scout helps the pack go.
Come to all the meetings.
Do what you can to help.
Think of others in the pack.

The pack helps the Cub Scout grow.
You can have fun when you are a part of the pack. Learn things from others. Do things with them.

The Cub Scout gives goodwill.
Smile. Be happy. Do things to help others. Little things make a big difference.

When you can say the Law of the Pack and tell what it means, fill in my track.

Akela's OK   Date   Recorded by the den leader

3 Tell what *Webelos* means.

Webelos

Webelos (say WE-buh-lows) has a special meaning that Cub Scouts know. It is <u>We</u>'ll <u>Be</u> <u>Lo</u>yal <u>S</u>couts.

We'll
Be
Loyal
Scouts
} **WeBeLoS**

Being loyal means that you will keep the Cub Scout Promise.

The Webelos Arrow of Light points the right way to go every day of the week. That is why the sun has seven rays—one for each day.

When you know what *Webelos* means, fill in my track.

Akela's OK   Date   Recorded by the den leader

4 Show the Cub Scout sign. Tell what it means.

Make the Cub Scout sign with your right hand. Hold with your arm straight up.

Cub Scout Sign

The two fingers stand for two parts of the Promise—"to help other people" and "to obey." They look like a wolf's ears ready to listen to Akela.

Give the Cub Scout sign when you say the Cub Scout Promise or the Law of the Pack.

When you can give the Cub Scout sign and tell what it means, fill in my track.

Akela's OK   Date   Recorded by the den leader

Cub Scout Handshake

Here's how to shake hands with another Cub Scout. Hold out your right hand just as you always do to shake hands. Put your first two fingers along the inside of the other boy's wrist.

This means that you help and that you obey the Law of the Pack.

When you can shake hands as a Cub Scout and tell what the handshake means, fill in my track.

Akela's OK   Date   Recorded by the den leader

Cub Scout Motto

DO YOUR BEST is the Cub Scout motto.

It means

When you play a game, do your best to help your team.

When you study in school, do your best to learn from your teacher.

When you help at home, do your best to help your family. Whatever you do, do your best.

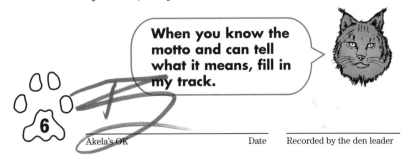

When you know the motto and can tell what it means, fill in my track.

6

Akela's OK   Date   Recorded by the den leader

7 Give the Cub Scout salute. Tell what it means.

Cub Scout Salute

A salute is a way to show respect. We salute the flag to show respect to our country.

For the Cub Scout salute, use your right hand. Hold your fingers as you do for the Cub Scout sign. Keep the two straight fingers close together. Touch the tips of those fingers to your cap. If you are not wearing a cap, touch your right eyebrow.

> When you can give the Cub Scout salute and tell what it means, fill in my track.

7 Akela's OK _____ Date _____ Recorded by the den leader

Child Protection Exercises

When you have completed these exercises with your parent or guardian, fill in my track.

8

Akela's OK   Date   Recorded by the den leader

Bobcat Trail

Fill in eight tracks to earn the Bobcat badge.

The Cub Scout Promise — 1

The Law of the Pack — 2

The Meaning of Webelos — 3

The Cub Scout Sign — 4

The Cub Scout Handshake — 5

The Cub Scout Motto — 6

The Cub Scout Salute — 7

Exercises in *How to Protect Your Children from Child Abuse* — 8

Your Den, Pack, and Uniform

A group of Cub Scouts, called a **den,** usually meets once a week in the same place. The dens all get together once a month for a pack meeting. Remember, as a Bear Cub Scout, you are a member of a pack. Remember, too, the Law of the Pack: "The Cub Scout helps the pack go." You should bring your whole family with you to each pack meeting. You will be proud not only to have them there to see you and your friends having fun but also to have them take part in the ceremony when you have earned a badge. The badge is given to an adult member of your family, and he or she will in turn give it to you in front of the whole pack. This is a way of saying "thank you" to your family for their help in earning your award.

Now that you are a Cub Scout in the Bear program, you have a blue neckerchief to wear with your Cub Scout uniform. Your Bear cap has a light blue front with the Bear emblem on it. If you don't wear your uniform to den and pack meetings, and on outings and special events, no one will be able to tell that you are a Cub Scout and that you have earned all the badges on your uniform shirt. Be proud to wear the Cub Scout uniform. Did you know there are Cub Scouts all around the world? You are a member of a large group of boys your age.

There are service stars, temporary patches (such as the World Conservation Award), Summertime Pack Award pins, Quality Unit emblems, and lots of other awards you can earn and wear on your uniform. (Ask your den leader to help you earn them and show you where each is worn.)

Turn to the very back of this book, inside the back cover, to see where to put the badges on your uniform.

Now, follow my

Bear Trail

You must complete twelve achievements to be a Bear Cub Scout. You can pick the ones you want to do from four different groups. You have a wide choice because there are twenty-four to pick from.

GOD (Do one.)
1. Ways We Worship
2. Emblems of Faith

COUNTRY (Do three.)
3. What Makes America Special?
4. Tall Tales
5. Sharing Your World with Wildlife
6. Take Care of Your Planet
7. Law Enforcement Is a Big Job

FAMILY (Do four.)
8. The Past Is Exciting and Important
9. What's Cooking?
10. Family Fun
11. Be Ready
12. Family Outdoor Adventures
13. Saving Well, Spending Well

SELF (Do four.)
14. Ride Right
15. Games, Games, Games! — *gon'*
16. Building Muscles

17. Information, Please
18. Jot It Down
19. Shavings and Chips
20. Sawdust and Nails
21. Build a Model
22. Tying It All Up
23. Sports, Sports, Sports
24. Be a Leader

When you finish an achievement, you will need to have an adult member of your family sign and date your book. You will then take your book to the next den meeting, and your den leader will record it on the Cub Scout Den Advancement Chart and initial your book.

When you have done 12 Bear achievements, you become a Bear Cub Scout. You will get your Bear badge from an adult member of your family at the pack meeting. Achievements that were not used to earn the Bear badge may be used as electives. However, note that unused parts of achievements that were used for the Bear badge may **not** be counted toward Arrow Points.

1 Ways We Worship

The people who wrote and signed our Constitution were very wise. They understood the need of Americans to worship God as they choose. A member of your family will be able to talk with you about your duty to God. Remember, this achievement is part of your Cub Scout Promise:

I,_____, promise to do my best to do my duty to God and my country. . ."

Complete both requirements.

REQUIREMENT

1a Complete the Character Connection for Faith.

Faith

practice

Know. Name some people in history who have shown great faith. Discuss with an adult how faith has been important at a particular point in his or her life.

Commit. Discuss with an adult how having faith and hope will help you in your life, and also discuss some ways that you can strengthen your faith.

Practice. Practice your faith as you are taught in your home, church, synagogue, mosque, or religious fellowship.

Many people throughout history have shown great faith while they worked to make our world a better world.

- It was Rabbi Menachem M. Schneersohn's (the Rebbe's) faith that saved thousands of his people, their culture, and their religion in Europe in the 1900s.
- The Reverend Dr. Martin Luther King Jr. relied on his faith as he led the Civil Rights movement in the 1960s.
- Mother Teresa's faith led her to help the poorest people and inspired people around the world to do what they could to help others, too.
- His Holiness the Dalai Lama, spiritual leader of the Tibetan people since 1950, has always worked for worldwide peace.

Akela's OK for the Bear Trail   Date

OR Akela's OK for the Arrow Point Trail   Date

Make a list of things you can do this week to practice your religion as you are taught in your home, church, synagogue, mosque, or other religious community. Check them off your list as you complete them.

I   worship

in song

in prayer

in study

and by kind and thoughtful acts toward others.

Akela's OK for the Bear Trail _____ Date

OR Akela's OK for the Arrow Point Trail _____ Date

CUB SCOUT LEADER BALOO SAYS: When you have done both of these requirements, have a parent or another adult sign here.

_____   _____   _____
Akela's OK   Date   Recorded by the den leader

Emblems of Faith

Many signs remind us of God. Among them are a six-pointed star, a cross, and a dove. There are many other religious symbols. One of them might appear on a special emblem you may earn and wear on your uniform. Contact your den leader, religious leader, or BSA local council service center for information about how to earn the award of your faith.

Learn more about your faith from your rabbi, minister, priest, imam, elder, or other religious leader.

Complete the requirement.

REQUIREMENT

2 Earn the religious emblem of your faith.

The Cub Scout who has earned the religious emblem of his faith may wear the religious emblems square knot on his uniform, above the left pocket, and he may continue to wear it as he advances in Scouting.

ALEPH
for Cub Scouts
who are Jewish

BISMILLAH
for Islamic
Cub Scouts

DHARMA
for Cub Scouts
who are Hindu

GOD AND COUNTRY
for Cub Scouts who are Christian
Scientist

GOD AND ME
for Cub Scouts of some Protestant
faiths

FAITH IN GOD
Church of Jesus Christ of Latter-day Saints
(religious emblems square knot)

JOYFUL SERVANT
for Cub Scouts
of the
Churches of Christ

LOVE FOR GOD
for Cub Scouts
of the Meher
Baba faith

LOVE OF GOD
for Polish National
Catholic Cub Scouts

METTA
for Cub Scouts who
are Buddhist

UNITY OF MANKIND
for Cub Scouts of the
Baha'i faith

SAINT GEORGE
for Eastern Orthodox
Cub Scouts

SAINT GREGORY
for Cub Scouts who are
members of the
Diocese of the
Armenian Church
of America
(Eastern Diocese)

THAT OF GOD
for Cub Scouts of the
Religious Society of
Friends (Quakers)

PARVULI DEI
for Cub Scouts who
are Roman Catholic or
Eastern-Rite Catholic
(grades 3–5)

Ask your den leader, religious leader, or local council service center for more information on religious emblems available to Cub Scouts.

CUB SCOUT LEADER BALOO SAYS: When you have done this requirement, have a parent or another adult sign here.

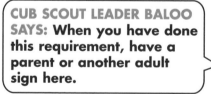

Akela's OK for the Bear Trail	Date	Recorded by the den leader
OR Akela's OK for the Arrow Point Trail	Date	Recorded by the den leader

3 Achievement

What Makes America Special?

Americans believe everyone should be free and should control his or her own life. We have the right to own property and to worship any way we want.

People did not always live this way. How men and women got together and started our free way of life makes an interesting story.

The story is still being written. Probably your parents and grandparents and even your great-grandparents are a part of it. You can be part of it, too.

As a Cub Scout, you can be one of the reasons that America is special. Help others. Be a good citizen. Take part in the life of your country.

Do requirements a and j and any two of the other requirements.

REQUIREMENT
3a   **Write or tell what makes America special to you.**

America, the beautiful, is special because of its

Opportunities

People

Freedom

a

Akela's OK for the Bear Trail   Date

OR Akela's OK for the Arrow Point Trail   Date

REQUIREMENT

3b

With the help of your family or den leader, find out about two famous Americans. Tell the things they did or are doing to improve our way of life.

Look for great Americans in

Books

Newspapers and magazines

TV programs about real people

There might be a great American living in your neighborhood or community.

b

Akela's OK for the Bear Trail   Date

OR Akela's OK for the Arrow Point Trail   Date

3c

Find out something about the old homes near where you live. Go to see two of them.

Akela's OK for the Bear Trail   Date

OR Akela's OK for the Arrow Point Trail   Date

3d

Find out where places of historical interest are located in or near your town or city. Go to visit one of them with your family or den.

These might be battlefields, monuments, or buildings or a place where early settlers lived or a famous story or poem was written.

Akela's OK for the Bear Trail   Date

OR Akela's OK for the Arrow Point Trail   Date

Achievement 3   **37**

3e Choose a state; it can be your favorite one or your home state. Name its state bird, tree, and flower. Describe its flag. Give the date it was admitted to the Union.

Use a reference book or Web site to find this information:

State bird_____

State tree_____

State flower_____

Date admitted to the union_____

MONTANA

Sketch your state flag.

e

_____
Akela's OK for the Bear Trail   Date

_____
OR Akela's OK for the Arrow Point Trail   Date

REQUIREMENT

3f Be a member of the color guard in a flag ceremony for your den or pack.

A color guard usually has four Cub Scouts. Numbers 1 and 4 are the guards. Number 2 carries the U.S. flag. Number 3 carries the den or pack flag.

f

_____
Akela's OK for the Bear Trail   Date

_____
OR Akela's OK for the Arrow Point Trail   Date

Memorial Day, the last Monday in May, honors those who died in defense of our country.

Flag Day, June 14, marks the day in 1777 when Congress adopted the Stars and Stripes as our flag.

Independence Day, July 4, celebrates the adoption of the Declaration of Independence, which marked the beginning of our nation's independence from Great Britain.

Veterans Day, November 11, honors the living veterans of all our wars. It is the anniversary of the end of World War I in 1918.

Labor Day, the first Monday in September, honors all working men and women.

_____

Akela's OK for the Bear Trail   Date

_____

OR Akela's OK for the Arrow Point Trail   Date

3h **Learn how to raise and lower a U.S. flag properly for an outdoor ceremony.**

Akela's OK for the Bear Trail   Date

OR Akela's OK for the Arrow Point Trail   Date

3i **Participate in an outdoor flag ceremony.**

Akela's OK for the Bear Trail   Date

OR Akela's OK for the Arrow Point Trail   Date

Complete the Character Connection for Citizenship.

Citizenship

practice

Know. Tell ways some people in the past have served our country. Tell about some people who serve our country today. (Don't forget about "ordinary" people who serve our country.)

Commit. Tell something that might happen to you and your family if other people were not responsible citizens. Tell one thing you will do to be a good citizen.

Practice. Tell three things you did in one week that show you are a good citizen.

Akela's OK for the Bear Trail _____ Date

OR Akela's OK for the Arrow Point Trail _____ Date

CUB SCOUT LEADER BALOO SAYS: When you have done requirements *a* and *j*, and two others, have a parent or another adult sign here.

3   Akela's OK _____ Date   Recorded by the den leader

Achievement

4 Tall Tales

A modern-day tall tale might be a fisherman's story about "the big one that got away." What we mean by "tall tales" in the *Bear Handbook* are stories, customs, songs, and sayings from our American past. These are handed down by families or groups of people. They tell us about the life and spirit of our ancestors. American folklore is told in stories and songs, some true and some told in a way to make the story better. One thing you can count on about tall tales or folklore is they tell about the happiness, fears, dreams, and hopes of early Americans. American folklore is full of wonderful people and adventures.

Do all three requirements.

REQUIREMENT

4a

Tell in your own words what folk-lore is. List some folklore stories, folk songs, or historical legends from your own state or part of the country. Play the Folklore Match Game on page 48.

SASQUATCH or BIGFOOT

A giant humanlike creature of the Pacific Northwest. Huge footprints and fleeting glimpses are all that anyone has seen of it.

PONY EXPRESS RIDERS

Between 1860 and 1861, riders carried the mail from Missouri to California. They rode at a gallop for 2,000 miles, changing horses every 10 miles.

PAUL BUNYAN

A tall-tales lumberman who leveled a forest with one swing of his ax. Then he trimmed the trees and stacked the logs for Babe, the blue ox, who swooshed them out of the woods in one haul.

PECOS BILL

A tall-tales cowboy who was raised by coyotes. He fought a 10-foot rattlesnake, tamed it, and used it as a whip. He caught and rode a mountain lion like a horse and he staked out New Mexico and dug the Grand Canyon.

RIP VAN WINKLE

The hero of Washington Irving's story about a man who went into the mountains to hunt. There he found a group of little men playing ninepins. He joined them and after the game laid down to take a nap, which lasted 20 years.

HIAWATHA

The main character of Longfellow's poem about an American Indian chief:

> You shall hear how Hiawatha
> Prayed and fasted in the forest,
> Not for triumphs in the battle,
> And renown among the warriors,
> But for profit of the people
> For advantage of the nations.

CHARLIE PARKHURST

A stagecoach driver before there were railroads. Charlie was unusual, because Charlie was a lady.

THE LOST DUTCHMAN

A mine, not a man, that is still lost. Somewhere in the Superstition Mountains of Arizona there is a hole in the ground loaded with gold.

JOHNNY APPLESEED

Jonathan Chapman was his real name. A Christian missionary who planted orchards in the wilderness, he was a friend of the American Indians and settlers. During the War of 1812 he saved the settlers from a surprise attack.

DANIEL BOONE

Hunter, pioneer, and trailblazer who led settlers over the Allegheny Mountains into Kentucky.

DAVY CROCKETT

Backwoods hero, member of Congress, and one of the defenders of the Alamo who died in its defense.

JOHN HENRY

A steel-driving champion whose record has never been equaled. In 35 minutes John Henry drove two 7-foot shafts into solid rock while a steam drill made only one 9-foot shaft.

ZORRO

A hero who lived on his father's hacienda (large ranch) in southern California when it was a colony of Mexico ruled by a governor who taxed and oppressed the people. Hiding his identity behind the mask of Zorro, Don Diego would ride to protect the cruel governor's victims.

EL DORADO

The American Indians told the Spaniards that somewhere in the West was a fabulous city of gold.

BARBARA FRITCHIE

Took up the flag hauled down by Confederate soldiers and defied Stonewall Jackson. "Shoot, if you must, this old gray head, but spare your country's flag," she said. A poem by John Greenleaf Whittier.

OLD STORMALONG

A tall-tales sailor who grew tired of the sea and said he was going to put his oar on his shoulder and walk west until someone asked: "What's that funny-looking stick on your shoulder?" There he vowed to settle down.

ICHABOD CRANE

An awkward schoolmaster in Washington Irving's "The Legend of Sleepy Hollow" who was scared out of town on Halloween night by the ghostly headless horseman (who was not really a ghost, but a jealous rival dressed as the horseman).

MOLLY BROWN

A tough frontier lady from the Colorado silver-mining town of Leadville who helped save some of the survivors of the *Titanic*.

KING KAMEHAMEHA

For 37 years, the ruler of Hawaii long before Hawaii was a part of the United States. He began his rule in 1782 and died in 1819.

CASEY JONES

A famous engineer who stayed with his train to warn others that it was going to crash. He died with one hand on the whistle and one hand on the brake. Old 638 crashed into a freight train that had not cleared the siding.

Folklore Match Game

1. Sasquatch or Bigfoot
2. Pony Express Riders
3. Paul Bunyan
4. Pecos Bill
5. Johnny Appleseed

6. Daniel Boone
7. Davy Crockett
8. John Henry

9. Zorro
10. El Dorado
11. Barbara Fritchie

12. Old Stormalong

13. Molly Brown
14. Ichabod Crane
15. Rip Van Winkle

16. Hiawatha
17. Charlie Parkhurst
18. Lost Dutchman
19. King Kamehameha

20. Casey Jones

___ Was of royal blood.
___ Slept a long time.
___ She drove a stagecoach.
___ Stood up to Stonewall.
___ Was frightened by some body.
___ Built of a precious metal.
___ Died in the Alamo.
___ From Leadville to the Titanic.
___ Got tired of the sea.
___ Beat a machine.
___ Protected victims of a cruel governor.
___ Warned the settlers of an attack.
___ Is famous in Kentucky.
___ A missing mine.
___ Leveled a forest with one swing of his ax.
___ Rode a strange "horse."
___ Longfellow's chief.
___ Stayed with his train.
___ Isn't a man, but a something.
___ Carried the mail.

Akela's OK for the Bear Trail   Date

OR Akela's OK for the Arrow Point Trail   Date

REQUIREMENT

 4b

Name at least five stories about American folklore. Point out on a United States map where they happened.

b

- Bunyan
- Big foot
- El dorado
- lost dutch
- Rip Van Winkle

REQUIREMENT

 4c

Read two folklore stories and tell your favorite one to your den.

Den leader's initials_____

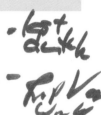
c

CUB SCOUT LEADER BALOO SAYS: When you have done all three requirements, have a parent or another adult sign here.

4

Akela's OK _____ Date _____ Recorded by the den leader

Achievement 4   49

Sharing Your World with Wildlife

Every living creature has a place in this world, and there is room for all of us. Birds, fish, and animals need clean water, food, and air, just as Cub Scouts do.

You can help protect wildlife by following the fishing and hunting laws. Keep wildlife areas beautiful. Pick up trash along trails, streams, and lakeshores. Put it in trash barrels where it belongs.

This achievement is also part of the Cub Scout World Conservation Award (see page 282).

NOTE for Akela: Ask your son's den leader to show you "Cub Scout Academics: Wildlife Conservation" in the *Cub Scout Academics and Sports Program Guide*.

Do four of the requirements.

Choose a bird or animal that you like and find out how it lives. Make a poster showing what you have learned.

Get to know birds or animals by

Reading about them

Watching them

_____

Akela's OK for the Bear Trail   Date

_____

OR Akela's OK for the Arrow Point Trail   Date

5b Build or make a bird feeder or birdhouse and hang it in a place where birds can visit safely.

Use white pine or cedar lumber. Do not use pressure-treated wood.

BIRDHOUSES

Birds that nest in the hollows of trees will nest in birdhouses. Six of the more common ones are bluebirds, chickadees, titmice, nuthatches, wrens, and house finches.

Birdhouse Sizes

BIRD	FLOOR	DEPTH	HOLE ABOVE FLOOR	HOLE SIZE	PLACE ABOVE GROUND
Bluebird	5x5 in.	8 in.	6 in.	1½ in.	5–10 ft.
Chickadee	4x4 in.	8–10 in.	6–8 in.	1½ in.	6–15 ft.
Titmouse	4x4 in.	8–10 in.	6–8 in.	1¼ in.	6–15 ft.
Nuthatch	4x4 in.	8–0 in	6–8 in.	1¼ in.	12–20 ft.
Wren	4x4 in.	6–8 in.	4–6 in.	1–1¼ in.	6–10 ft.
House finch	6x6 in.	6 in.	4 in.	2 in.	8–12 ft.

Akela's OK for the Bear Trail _____ Date

OR Akela's OK for the Arrow Point Trail _____ Date

5c Explain what a wildlife conservation officer does.

Contact a conservation officer from your state or federal fish and wildlife service. Look in your phone book. Tell the officer that you are a Cub Scout and are working on this achievement. The person you talk with might be one or more of these three things:

RESEARCHER

Studies the lives and habits of wild animals and birds. Finds out how wild things live, where they live, what they eat, what eats them, how they raise babies, and how they survive during the winter.

MANAGER

Helps provide wild animals with things they need—food, water, shelter, and living space.

EDUCATOR

Writes books or articles for newspapers about wildlife. He or she might be on radio or TV shows, make movies, or give talks to Cub Scout packs or school classes on wildlife.

Akela's OK for the Bear Trail   Date

OR Akela's OK for the Arrow Point Trail   Date

5d   Visit one of the following:

_____ Zoo   _____ Wildlife refuge
_____ Nature center   _____ Game preserve
_____ Aviary

Find out if any of these places are near your home. Take a trip to one of them with your family or den.

Akela's OK for the Bear Trail   Date

OR Akela's OK for the Arrow Point Trail   Date

5e Name one animal that has become extinct in the last 100 years. Tell why animals become extinct. Name one animal that is on the endangered species list.

Talk with a conservation officer or librarian.

Akela's OK for the Bear Trail   Date

OR Akela's OK for the Arrow Point Trail   Date

CUB SCOUT LEADER BALOO SAYS: When you have done four requirements, have a parent or another adult sign here.

5 Akela's OK   Date   Recorded by the den leader

Take Care of Your Planet

Achievement 6

The Earth is your planet. This means that you have to help take care of it. It's the only planet we have. Conserve energy. Save our natural resources. Plant trees and flowers.

Do three of the requirements.

Achievement 6

Take Care of Your Planet

The Earth is your planet. This means that you have to help take care of it. It's the only planet we have. Conserve energy. Save our natural resources. Plant trees and flowers.

Do three of the requirements.

Save 5 pounds of glass or aluminum or 1 month of daily newspapers. Turn them in at a recycling center or use your community's recycling service.

Stack and tie newspapers according to local recycling rules.

Separate your trash at home according to local recycling rules.

Find out if some bottles and cans may be returned for a cash deposit. Rinse bottles and cans to be recycled and crush cans to save space.

Akela's OK for the Bear Trail   Date

OR Akela's OK for the Arrow Point Trail   Date

6b Plant a tree in your yard, on the grounds of the group that operates your Cub Scout pack, or in a park or other public place. Be sure to get permission first.

Trees make buildings more attractive and help them stay cooler in summer.

Planting Seedlings

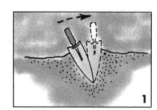

1. Push the trowel into the ground, and then push the handle up straight.

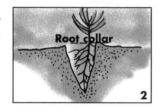

Root collar

2. Remove the trowel and place the seedling with its root collar at ground level.

3. Push the trowel into the ground 2 inches from the seedling. Push the handle away from the plant. This will firm the soil at the bottom of the roots.

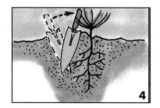

4. Now pull the handle toward the plant to firm the soil at the top of the roots.

5. Fill in the trowel hole by scraping the soil with your foot.

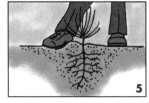

6. Pack the soil firmly around the seedling with your foot.

Some seedlings will be taller than you are in 5 years. You will be able to sit in their shade in 10 years.

Akela's OK for the Bear Trail   Date

OR Akela's OK for the Arrow Point Trail   Date

REQUIREMENT
6c **Call city or county officials or your trash-hauling company and find out what happens to your trash after it is hauled away.**

Is any of it
- Recycled?
- Burned to generate electricity?

If it is dumped and buried in a landfill, what will happen to the land afterward?

Akela's OK for the Bear Trail   Date

OR Akela's OK for the Arrow Point Trail   Date

List all the ways water is used in your home. Search for dripping faucets or other ways water might be wasted. With an adult, repair or correct those problems.

———— Cooking   ———— Garden

———— Dish washing   ———— Shrubs and trees

———— Laundry   ———— Swimming pool

———— Showers and baths   ———— Drinking

———— Toilets   ———— Fountains

———— Lawn   ———— Hobbies

How to Repair a Leaky Faucet

1. With an adult, locate the shutoff valve for the faucet. Turn off the water.
2. Protect the finish of the packing nut by wrapping it with a soft cloth.
3. Loosen the packing nut carefully. Turn and lift out the stem assembly.
4. Remove the screw at the bottom of the stem assembly. Pry out the old washer. Clean out the place where it was.
5. Replace the worn washer with one that fits. Insert flat side down. Replace the screw.
6. Wipe the valve seat clean. Replace the stem assembly. Wrap the soft cloth around the packing nut again, and then carefully tighten it. Turn on the valve. Test the faucet.

Akela's OK for the Bear Trail   Date

_____

OR Akela's OK for the Arrow Point Trail   Date

6e Discuss with an adult in your family the kinds of energy your family uses.

―――― Solar   ―――― Diesel fuel
―――― Wind   ―――― Electricity
―――― Natural gas   ―――― Wood
―――― Propane   ―――― Kerosene
―――― Gasoline   ―――― Charcoal briquettes
―――― Heating oil   ――― ――――――――――
                                        (other)

Akela's OK for the Bear Trail   Date

OR Akela's OK for the Arrow Point Trail   Date

REQUIREMENT

6f Find out more about your family's use of electricity.

Visit or call your power company for help in completing this requirement. Ask how electricity is generated for your home.

Check off the appliances your family has and underline the ones that use a lot of electricity:

———— Toaster   ———— Fan
———— Stove   ———— Water heater
———— Microwave   ———— Dishwasher
———— Refrigerator   ———— Washing machine
———— Heater   ———— Clothes dryer
———— Radio   ———— Hair dryer
———— TV   ———— Iron
———— Clock   ———— _____
———— Computer   (other)
———— Air conditioning unit   ———— _____
                                     (other)

To save electricity:

- Turn off lights when no one is using them.

- Turn off the TV when no one is watching.

- Don't turn the thermostat too warm in winter or too cool in summer.

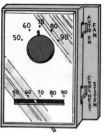

Winter

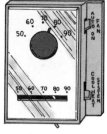

Summer

Akela's OK for the Bear Trail   Date

OR Akela's OK for the Arrow Point Trail   Date

REQUENT

6g Take part in a den or pack neighborhood clean-up project.

Akela's OK for the Bear Trail   Date

OR Akela's OK for the Arrow Point Trail   Date

CUB SCOUT LEADER BALOO SAYS: When you have done three of these requirements, have a parent or another adult sign here.

Akela's OK   Date   Recorded by the den leader

7 Law Enforcement Is a Job

Police officers need our help as they work to protect us. We need to understand ways of taking care of ourselves. Crime has always been a problem everywhere. But we can do something about it. This achievement will help you understand how the police and others fight crime. It will also show you ways that you can help.

Do all six requirements.

Practice one way police gather evidence: by taking fingerprints, or taking shoeprints, or taking tire track casts.

Police look for fingerprints at the scene of a crime so that when they arrest someone, they can compare that person's prints against the ones found at the crime scene. If the prints match, it may prove that the person was there, because no one has prints just like anyone else's.

Make a set of your fingerprints and a set of an adult's fingerprints. Look at them closely. What differences do you see?

This is how to make a set of fingerprints:

Use an ink pad. Press your finger on the pad and then on a piece of paper. When you can get a good, sharp print, make your set of prints right here in the book.

Your Fingerprints

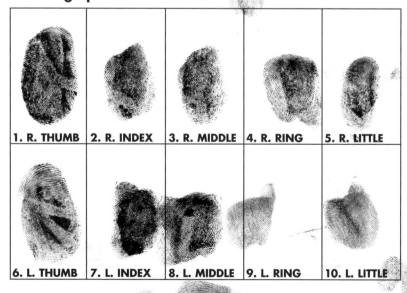

1. R. THUMB	2. R. INDEX	3. R. MIDDLE	4. R. RING	5. R. LITTLE
6. L. THUMB	7. L. INDEX	8. L. MIDDLE	9. L. RING	10. L. LITTLE

Adult's Fingerprints

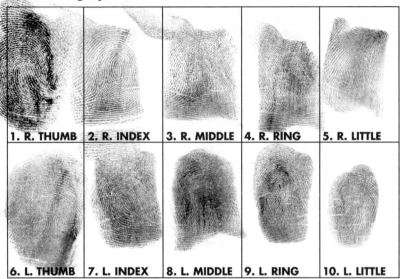

1. R. THUMB	2. R. INDEX	3. R. MIDDLE	4. R. RING	5. R. LITTLE
6. L. THUMB	7. L. INDEX	8. L. MIDDLE	9. L. RING	10. L. LITTLE

A shoe or tire track print can be evidence, too. Police make casts of prints found at the scene of the crime and then compare them to brands of shoes or tires; if suspects own that brand, it shows they *might* have been there. If there is something unique—such as a cut across the sole or a bit of tread missing—it can prove they *were* there.

Here is how you can work with an adult to make a shoe or tire track print:

Make a plaster cast of a shoeprint.

Make a good, clear track in sand or soft earth. Put a cardboard ring around it.

Mix water with plaster of paris until it's like thin pudding. Pour it over the track and let it harden.

Pick up the hardened plaster. Clean off any dirt that has stuck to it. Compare the sole of the shoe or tire that made the track to the plaster shoeprint.

Akela's OK for the Bear Trail	Date

OR Akela's OK for the Arrow Point Trail	Date

REQUIREMENT

7b

Visit your local sheriff's office or police station or talk with a law enforcement officer visiting your den or pack to discuss crime prevention.

Meet a deputy sheriff or police officer who patrols your neighborhood.

Akela's OK for the Bear Trail	Date

OR Akela's OK for the Arrow Point Trail	Date

With an adult in your family, check to be sure you have tight, strong locks on your doors and windows.

A deadbolt should be more than 1 inch long.

Until you can install a lock, place a board in the frame to keep a sliding door or window from being forced open.

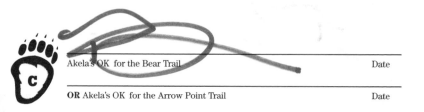

Akela's OK for the Bear Trail   Date

OR Akela's OK for the Arrow Point Trail   Date

REQUIREMENT

7d Be sure you know where to get help in your neighborhood.

With your parent or guardian, get to know the people in your neighborhood who can help you in an emergency. Make a list of those people and their phone numbers.

Name Lawerence + Nora

Address

Phone

Name Jessica's house.

Address

Phone

Name Krausers.

Address

Phone

Name

Address

Phone

Akela's OK for the Bear Trail — Date

OR Akela's OK for the Arrow Point Trail — Date

Learn the phone numbers to use in an emergency and post them by each phone in your home.

Check your phone book to see if your community has 911 service. If it does, learn when you should and when you should not call 911 and check to see if there are other emergency service numbers that you should know. If you don't have 911 service, find the numbers for law enforcement, fire, and other emergency services.

Make a list of your community's emergency phone numbers and post it (and your neighborhood emergency help list) near all phones in your house. Memorize these numbers and practice dialing them with your eyes closed.

Police _____ 911 _____

Fire _____ 911 _____

Medical _____ 911 _____

Poison control center _____ 911 _____

Other _____

_____
Akela's OK for the Bear Trail   Date

_____
OR Akela's OK for the Arrow Point Trail   Date

7f Know what you can do to help law enforcement.

If you see a crime being committed or some dangerous activity, tell an adult or call the police.

Get the facts:
- Where is it happening?
- What's happening?
- Who is doing it?
  —Can you describe the people and their clothes?
  —Did you get the license number?

Don't put yourself in danger!
Get all the information you can,
then tell an adult or call the police.

Akela's OK for the Bear Trail _____ Date

OR Akela's OK for the Arrow Point Trail _____ Date

CUB SCOUT LEADER BALOO SAYS: When you have done all six requirements, have a parent or another adult sign here.

Akela's OK _____ Date _____ Recorded by the den leader

8 The Past Is Exciting and Important

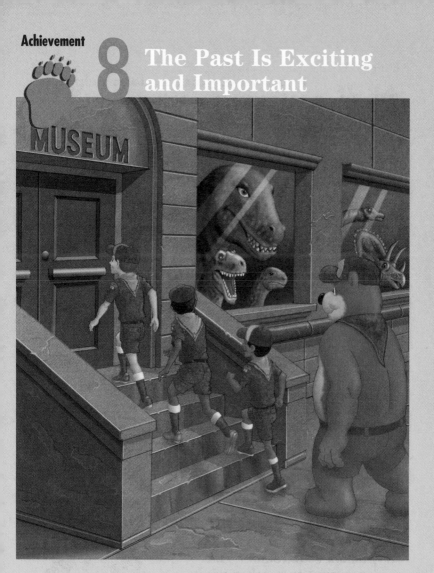

Something that happened 100 years ago can seem as exciting and interesting as something that happened yesterday.

You learn about America's past in school. Your family has a history, too; so has your community and your Cub Scout pack.

Do requirement g and two other requirements.

Visit your library or newspaper office. Ask to see back issues of newspapers or an almanac.

What was happening in the world

- When you were born?

_____

_____

- On July 20, 1969?

_____

_____

- When you were 5 years old?

_____

_____

Akela's OK for the Bear Trail   Date

_____

OR Akela's OK for the Arrow Point Trail   Date

Achievement 8   **73**

Find someone who was a Cub Scout a long time ago. Talk with him about what Cub Scouting was like then.

What did he do at
• Den meetings?

_____

_____

_____

• Pack meetings?

_____

_____

_____

What kind of uniform did he wear?

_____

_____

_____

_____

_____

Akela's OK for the Bear Trail   Date

OR Akela's OK for the Arrow Point Trail   Date

8c **Start or add to an existing den or pack scrapbook.**

You might add a
- Picture
- Pack meeting program in which you took part
- Newspaper from your school
- Report on a Good Turn or service project done by your den or pack

Akela's OK for the Bear Trail   Date

OR Akela's OK for the Arrow Point Trail   Date

Trace your family back through your grandparents or great-grandparents; or talk to a grandparent about what it was like when he or she was younger.

What did he or she do
- At school?
- During holidays?
- At home to help around the house?

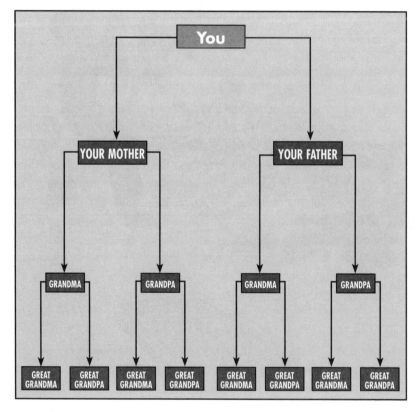

Akela's OK for the Bear Trail   Date

OR Akela's OK for the Arrow Point Trail   Date

8e **Find out some history about your community.**

Perhaps you can talk to someone who has lived in your community for a long time or visit a local museum to learn things like:

- How did people heat their homes?
- Where was the first school?
- Where was the fire station?
- Where were the places of worship?

You might find some books about the history of your community in your library.

Akela's OK for the Bear Trail   Date

OR Akela's OK for the Arrow Point Trail   Date

8f **Start your own history: keep a journal for 2 weeks.**

Jot down some of the things you do each day. When you grow up, you can share what it was like when you were a Cub Scout.

Akela's OK for the Bear Trail   Date

OR Akela's OK for the Arrow Point Trail   Date

8g **Complete the Character Connection for Respect.**

Respect

Know. As you learn about what Cub Scout–age life was like for adults you know, does what you learn change what you think about them? Tell how it might help you respect or value them more.

Commit. Can you think of reasons others might be disrespectful to people or things you value? Name one new way you will show respect for a person or thing someone else values.

Practice. List some ways you can show respect for people and events in the past.

Akela's OK for the Bear Trail   Date

OR Akela's OK for the Arrow Point Trail   Date

CUB SCOUT LEADER BALOO SAYS: When you have done requirement g and two other requirements, have a parent or another adult sign here.

8

_____   _____
Akela's OK   Date   Recorded by the den leader

What's Cooking?

We all like to eat good things. Good things seem to taste even better when we make them ourselves. In this achievement you will want to work with someone who knows how to cook. You and that person can cook up some great food.

Do not try to do any of these requirements unless an adult is helping you!

Do four requirements.

9a   With an adult, bake cookies.

How to Make Oatmeal Cookies

Preheat oven to 350°F.

¾ cup vegetable shortening
1 cup firmly packed brown sugar
½ cup granulated sugar
1 egg
¼ cup water
1 teaspoon vanilla
3 cups uncooked oatmeal
1 cup all-purpose flour
1 teaspoon salt (optional)
½ teaspoon baking soda

Beat together the shortening, sugars, egg, water, and vanilla until creamy. Combine the remaining ingredients, add to the first mixture, and mix well. Drop by rounded teaspoonfuls onto a greased cookie sheet. Bake at 350°F for 12 to 15 minutes. For variety, add chopped nuts, raisins, chocolate chips, or coconut. Makes about 60 cookies.

If you don't like oatmeal cookies, use another recipe from a cookbook. Or use a packaged mix and follow the directions on the package.

_____
Akela's OK for the Bear Trail   Date

_____
OR Akela's OK for the Arrow Point Trail   Date

9b With an adult, make snacks for the next den meeting.

HARD-BOILED EGGS

Place eggs in a cooking pot or pan. Cover with cold water. Bring the water to a full boil. Reduce the heat and simmer for 15 minutes. Drain the hot water and replace it with cold. Drain and let the eggs dry. Put them in the refrigerator until you're ready to eat them. The egg is perfectly packaged by nature for picnics.

CARROT AND CELERY STICKS

Brush carrots and celery clean. Pare off dark spots. Cut off tops and bottoms. Cut in half lengthwise. Cut the half strips in quarters. Then cut into sticks.

POPCORN

Under the supervision of an adult, make popcorn. You might want to make it the "old-fashioned" way: Pour enough cooking oil into a large pan to cover the bottom. Add corn, spreading it so that each kernel is touching the bottom. Place the pan on medium-high heat and cover it with a tight-fitting lid. Gently shake the pan throughout popping so the corn won't burn. When the popping stops, remove the pan from the heat and pour the popcorn into a bowl. Add melted butter or margarine. Salt to taste.

Akela's OK for the Bear Trail   Date

OR Akela's OK for the Arrow Point Trail   Date

With an adult prepare one part of your breakfast, one part of your lunch, and one part of your supper.

JUICE

Squeeze fresh oranges, or you can use frozen orange juice or a mix. Follow the directions on the can or the package.

COOKED CEREAL

Follow the directions on the package.

SANDWICHES AND SOUP

This combination makes a good lunch any time of the year. Use canned soup or a mix. Follow the directions on the can or package. Make your sandwiches with whatever you have. Luncheon meat, cheese slices, sliced tomatoes, lettuce, and mayonnaise make a super sandwich. You don't need to have all of that in one sandwich. You could make three different kinds. Peanut butter and jelly also make a good sandwich. Spread peanut butter on one slice of bread and jelly on the other. Put the two to-gether and slice in half. Replace the jar covers and clean the spreading knife.

BOILED POTATOES

Scrub enough potatoes for your family. (One for each person is about right.) Some families peel their potatoes, but others like the flavor of the whole potato. Do this the way your family likes. Cut them in quarters. Put the potatoes in a pan and add enough water to cover them. Add ¼ teaspoon of salt. Cover the pan. Bring the water to a boil, and then reduce the heat. Cook for 20 minutes or until you can easily push a fork into a potato. Remove from the heat. Drain the water, using the cover to keep the potatoes from spilling out. Replace on the heat for about 10 seconds to dry. Serve with butter, margarine, or gravy.

TASTY VEGETABLES

Most vegetables taste best when steamed or cooked with only a little water. Clean green beans, broccoli, carrots, or asparagus well, then with an adult, steam them or cook them in a pan with a few tablespoons of water, just until they are done.

SPAGHETTI

Follow the directions on the package. Heat bottled sauce to eat with your spaghetti.

Akela's OK for the Bear Trail _____ Date _____

OR Akela's OK for the Arrow Point Trail _____ Date _____

9d   Make a list of the "junk foods" you eat. Discuss "junk food" with a parent or teacher.

Junk foods have too many calories and too few nutrients. Foods with a lot of sugar might not have the vitamins and minerals you need.

- Soft drinks
- Candy
- Ice cream
- Chips

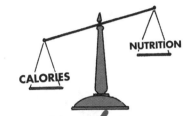

NUTRITION

CALORIES

CHIPS

CANDY

BIG BAR

Handwritten notes: Candy, pep — g h chips, cat pit

_____/_____Date and teacher's signature

Akela's OK for the Bear Trail _____ Date

d

OR Akela's OK for the Arrow Point Trail _____ Date

Achievement 9   **85**

9e   Make some trail food for a hike.

NUTS AND BOLTS
Mix peanuts and raisins together with some dry cereal.

Note: If preparing trail mix for a hike, check to be sure that there are no food allergies among den members, especially to peanuts.

Akela's OK for the Bear Trail   Date

OR Akela's OK for the Arrow Point Trail   Date

REQUIREMENT

9f With an adult, make a dessert for your family.

INSTANT PUDDING
Empty the contents of the package into a bowl. Follow the directions on the package.

BROWNIES
Follow the directions on the package.

FLAVORED GELATIN
Follow the directions on the package. It's even better if you add some fruit!

Akela's OK for the Bear Trail	Date
OR Akela's OK for the Arrow Point Trail	Date

9g With an adult, cook something outdoors.

Work on your outdoor cooking skills with a family favorite, or try one of these:

Pigs in Blankets

Wrap a hot dog in biscuit dough (from a can or a mix). Wrap in foil and place over coals on a grill. Turn every 3 or 4 minutes. It will be done in about 15 minutes.

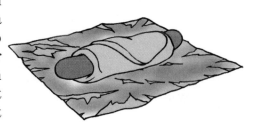

S'Mores

For each person, place a piece of chocolate bar on a graham cracker. Put a marshmallow on a long-handled fork or stick and toast it over coals or a fire. When golden brown, put the marshmallow on the chocolate and top with another graham cracker.

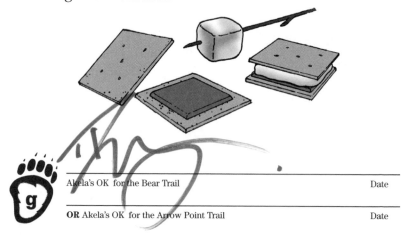

Akela's OK for the Bear Trail _____ Date

OR Akela's OK for the Arrow Point Trail _____ Date

CUB SCOUT LEADER BALOO SAYS: When you have done four of these requirements, have a parent or another adult sign here.

9

_____   _____   _____
Akela's OK   Date   Recorded by the den leader

10 Family Fun

A family is people who care for each other, and have fun together. Plan a day trip or an evening out. Have a family night at home to plan your outing.

A parent or guardian is like Baloo, a Cub Scout leader who can show you many useful and interesting things.

Do both requirements.

10a Go on a day trip or evening out with members of your family.

You could visit one of the following:

_____ Park   _____ Airport   _____ Farm or
_____ Museum   _____ Seashore   ranch

BEFORE YOU GO.

Think of the things that you might need, and pack them in a handy bag. Your needs might differ according to how you are traveling (by car, train, bus, subway, ferry, or bicycle or on foot).

TRAVEL BEHAVIOR AND SAFETY.

If your trip will be by car, an adult family member should make sure the car is safe to drive before the trip begins.

You will be expected to get yourself ready and agree to

- Buckle yourself in with a seat belt. Urge others to use theirs; in many states, it's the law. Make sure infants and small children ride in approved car seats and that only adults ride in front.
- Change seats only at roadside stops. Don't climb from one seat to another while the car is moving.
- Keep your hands and arms inside the car.
- Keep doors locked at all times.
- Keep all windows closed whenever possible. Never drive with a rear window open.
- Save paper and trash for roadside barrels. Don't litter.
- Pack everything in the trunk or carrier except snacks, game bag, and books.

- Don't be noisy or shout inside the car. Noise can bother the driver and could cause an accident.

If your trip includes travel on a bus, train, subway, ferry, or other public means of transportation, follow these simple rules to keep your trip a safe and fun one:
- Use good manners and be considerate of others.
- Always stay with an adult in your group.
- Before you go, learn the rules for this kind of travel. Obey them and all posted signs.
- Don't be noisy or shout inside the vehicle.

WHAT TO DO FOR A TRIP IN TOWN
Find out what time tours are given at a museum or other place of interest. Ask if a reservation is required. Arrive on time. Stay with your group. (But know what you should do if separated from the group.) Treat your guide with respect. Listen to what he or she says. Keep the noise down—be polite.

Akela's OK for the Bear Trail _____ Date

OR Akela's OK for the Arrow Point Trail _____ Date

10b Have a family fun night at home.

Play a favorite game with your family, and practice good sportsmanship. Or you could get together to make a home-made game, something useful for your house, or holiday decorations.

BOOT JACK

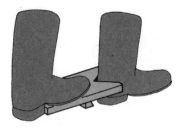

Make it easy to take off your boots or overshoes. Any piece of 1-inch-thick scrap wood that is 1 foot long and 3 inches wide will do. Cut a V in one end.

Then nail a short piece of wood beneath the point of the V.

BULLETIN BOARD

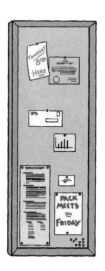

A long narrow bulletin board is easy for all members of the family to read. Put the grown-ups' notices at the top and the children's at the bottom. Start with a panel from a corrugated box. Cover it with plain cloth. Tack it to a narrow wooden frame.

Akela's OK for the Bear Trail _____ Date

OR Akela's OK for the Arrow Point Trail _____ Date

CUB SCOUT LEADER BALOO SAYS: When you have completed both requirements, have a parent or another adult sign here.

10

_____   _____   _____
Akela's OK   Date   Recorded by the den leader

11 Be Ready

You can expect firefighters, police officers, and paramedics to help and protect you in an emergency. Sometimes, though, you have to take care of yourself or someone else until help arrives. You should be ready to do the right thing if this happens.

Fires and accidents can be frightening, and it is natural to be scared. That is why we think about what to do before an emergency happens.

In a very serious case, there is little time to stop and figure out what to do. That is why we must be ready. If someone's clothes are on fire, or breathing has stopped, you must act at once. In other emergencies there might be time to stop a few seconds and think about what to do.

Your best way to handle most emergencies is to get help from an adult.

A good way to be ready is to carry enough change for a pay phone. Some pay phones don't require money to reach an operator—you just press "0." In some areas you can dial 911 for help. Find out if you can do that where you live.

Do requirements _a_ through _e_ and requirement _g_. Requirement _f_ is recommended, but not required.

REQUIREMENT

11a Tell what to do in case of an accident in the home. A family member needs help. Someone's clothes catch on fire.

What should you do if you are at home with a family member and he or she falls down the stairs or off of a ladder and gets hurt? Talk it over with an adult and think about these things:

1. Be calm and make the person as comfortable as possible without moving him or her. Don't try to move an injured person. You might make the injury worse if you do.

2. GET HELP! If there is someone in the yard or nearby, send that person to get a neighbor or call for an ambulance. Do it yourself if no one else is around.

3. Stay with the injured person. Use a blanket to keep him or her warm.

What should you do if someone's clothes catch on fire? Find out. Talk it over with an adult.

1. Usually a person panics and starts to run—stop him! Running fans the flames and makes them spread.

2. If the person can be caught, force him or her to the ground or floor. Roll the victim over and over to smother the flames. Wrap them with a rug, blanket, or sweater, working from the neck down. If you can't catch the victim, yell "Stop! Stop! Stop!," and then throw yourself on the ground and roll so the victim can see you and do what you do. **Cover your face so the victim will, too.**

3. As soon as you can, help the person get to a place where the burned parts of the body can be covered with clean dressings and treated by a doctor.

What should you do if your own clothes catch on fire?

1. **Stop** where you are. **Don't run!**
2. Drop to the floor or ground.
3. Roll and cover your face.
4. If you are indoors, grab a rug, blanket, or coat and wrap yourself as you roll. Start at your neck.

What should you do if your house catches on fire?

1. First, get everyone out of the house! Crawl along the floor to avoid breathing smoke.
2. Don't try to put the fire out yourself.
3. Call the fire department from a neighbor's house.
4. When the firefighters arrive, let them know everyone is out of the house.

> **Remember: Never go back into a burning building for any reason.**

Akela's OK for the Bear Trail   Date

OR Akela's OK for the Arrow Point Trail   Date

11b Tell what to do in case of a water accident.

A boat overturns and you are in it. What do you do?

1. **Don't panic.** Grab the boat and stay with it.

2. Help the other passengers to find a place where they can hold on. **No one should try to swim ashore.** Stay with the boat; it will support you. Wait for rescuers.

3. If the boat can be turned right side up, get inside and sit as low as possible on the bottom.

Someone slips off a bank into the water. What do you do?

1. Reach the person, if possible, with your hand or leg. Take off your sweater or shirt and toss one end to the person. You can also extend a stick, fishing pole, branch, or anything that is handy.
2. Throw something to the person that will float, such as a cushion, inner tube, plank, or a ring buoy, if available.

Someone falls through the ice. What do you do?

1. Remember, if you get too close, you might break through, too.
2. Find something to throw to the person.
3. Look around for a ladder, a long branch, or anything you can use to reach toward the person. Lie flat on safe ice and push the item toward the person until he or she can grab it. Then you can pull him or her out.
4. When the person is out of the water, get him or her to someplace warm.

See "Boats," elective 5 on the Arrow Point trail (page 196), for more information about water safety.

Akela's OK for the Bear Trail   Date

OR Akela's OK for the Arrow Point Trail   Date

11c **Tell what to do in case of a school bus accident.**

1. Always know where emergency exits are whenever you get on a bus.

2. In case of an accident, follow directions from the driver. If the driver is injured, stay calm. Tell others to take it easy and get out of the bus through the emergency exits. Move to the side of the road, away from traffic.

3. Help the bus driver get everyone out without pushing.

Akela's OK for the Bear Trail   Date

OR Akela's OK for the Arrow Point Trail   Date

 11d **Tell what to do in case of a car accident.**

1. Be calm. Help the adults by doing what you are told.

2. Suggest to the driver that the car be left where it is until the police come. Ask an adult to direct traffic around it.

3. Don't go out into the road yourself. Watch for other cars. All passengers should get out of the car on the side away from traffic.

4. Don't move anyone who might be badly injured.

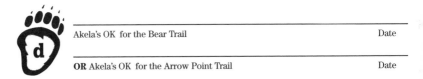

Akela's OK for the Bear Trail _____ Date

OR Akela's OK for the Arrow Point Trail _____ Date

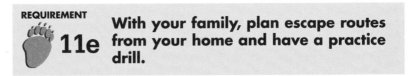

REQUIREMENT

11e With your family, plan escape routes from your home and have a practice drill.

Be sure everyone in the family knows how to escape from every room in the house!

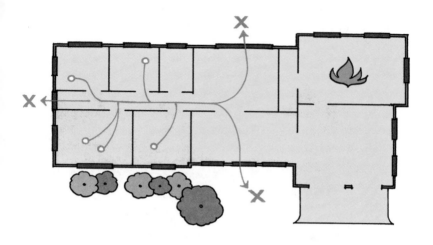

Akela's OK for the Bear Trail _____ Date _____

OR Akela's OK for the Arrow Point Trail _____ Date _____

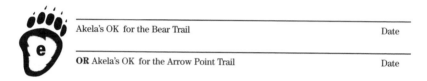

REQUIREMENT

11f **Have a health checkup by a physician (optional).**

RECOMMENDED, BUT NOT REQUIRED. A health checkup is a good thing to have each year. It will show you what to do for your health's sake.

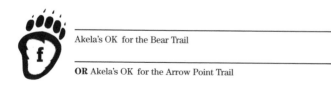

Akela's OK for the Bear Trail _____ Date _____

OR Akela's OK for the Arrow Point Trail _____ Date _____

11g **Complete the Character Connection for Courage.**

Courage

Know. Memorize the courage steps: Be brave, Be calm, Be clear, and Be careful. Tell why each courage step is important. How will memorizing the courage steps help you to be ready?

Commit. Tell why it might be difficult to follow the courage steps in an emergency situation. Think of other times you can use the courage steps. (Standing up to a bully is one example.)

Practice. Act out one of the requirements using these courage steps: Be brave, Be calm, Be clear, and Be careful.

Akela's OK for the Bear Trail   Date

OR Akela's OK for the Arrow Point Trail   Date

CUB SCOUT LEADER BALOO SAYS:
When you have done requirements a through e and requirement g—requirement f is recommended, but not required—have a parent or another adult sign here.

Akela's OK   Date   Recorded by the den leader

12 Family Outdoor Adventures

You might live in a state that has snow in winter, or you might live where it is warm all the time. No matter where you live, being outside and doing things with your family is great. You can have fun together and get to know one another better.

Do three requirements.

NOTE for Akela: This achievement is required for both the Cub Scout Leave No Trace Awareness Award and the Cub Scout Outdoor Activity Award. See pages 283–285 for the requirements for both awards.

12a Go camping with your family.

CAMPING

When you spend time outdoors and stay overnight in a tent, camper, trailer, or motor home, that's camping. Be sure to help your family pack for the trip. You will need to be ready

for changes in the weather. It can get cold at night or rain suddenly. Pack things that keep you warm and dry.

Akela's OK for the Bear Trail   Date

OR Akela's OK for the Arrow Point Trail   Date

12b Go on a hike with your family.

HIKING

A hike is more than a walk. When you hike, you go exploring to find out something. You can hike in the city; forest preserves; county, state, or national parks; or even the zoo. **Never hike alone.**

KEEPING DRY

When you are far from shelter, what will you do when it rains? Some smart outdoor families have

PLASTIC BAGS

1 GALLON FOOD STORAGE BAG RAIN HAT

Cut

Cut

30 GALLON TRASH BAG PONCHO

solved that problem. Each family member carries a plastic trash-bag poncho. When it rains, just slip it over your head and wear it like a sleeveless sweater. You can also make a rain cap from a plastic food-storage bag.

Keep away from hilltops and trees that could draw lightning.

SUN SAFETY

Too much sun can be dangerous. Follow these tips from the

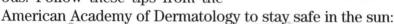

American Academy of Dermatology to stay safe in the sun:

- Try to stay out of the sun between 10 A.M. and 4 P.M. when the sun's rays are the strongest.
- Use lots of sunscreen with a sun protection factor (SPF) of at least 15. Put on more every two hours when you're outdoors, even on cloudy days.
- Wear protective, tightly woven clothing, such as a long-sleeved shirt and pants.
- Wear a 4-inch-wide broad-brimmed hat and sunglasses with lenses that protect you against the sun's ultraviolet rays (called UV protection).
- Stay in the shade whenever you can.
- Stay away from reflective surfaces, which can reflect up to 85 percent of the sun's damaging rays.

DON'T GET LOST!

Stay with your family. Don't wander off by yourself. Carry a police whistle to signal for help if you get lost. Three sharp blasts on your whistle means "Emergency!"

LEAVE YOUR TRACKS.

Even with careful planning and with clear instructions to follow the buddy plan, sometimes a hiker can become separated from the group. When hikers are lost, searchers need to know what their tracks look like. Before setting out on a hike into the woods, have the hikers in your group leave their tracks. Here's how to leave your tracks: Fold a soft towel until it is roughly the size of your hiking shoes. Place the folded towel on a newspaper and cover it with a piece of aluminum foil. Stand on the foil and step off. The print you make can help searchers find you if necessary. Write the color of your clothes on a slip of paper and leave it with your footprint.

Tell someone where your group is going and when you will return. Give that person the aluminum foil tracks of all

the hiking shoes. If someone gets separated from the group or if the group doesn't get back on time, that person can alert the authorities and give them the information they need for their search.

STAY WHERE YOU ARE.

If you ever think you are lost, sit down and wait in the open where people can see you. Searchers will find you. **Don't try to find your way back**

Akela's OK for the Bear Trail   Date

OR Akela's OK for the Arrow Point Trail   Date

12c Have a picnic with your family.

How about a breakfast picnic?

How about an all-star favorite-food roundup? That's when everyone brings his or her favorite food to share with others.

_____

Akela's OK for the Bear Trail   Date

_____

OR Akela's OK for the Arrow Point Trail   Date

12d Attend an outdoor event with your family.

A hot-air balloon race

A bird count

A fish derby

A craft fair

Akela's OK for the Bear Trail	Date
OR Akela's OK for the Arrow Point Trail	Date

 12e Plan your outdoor family day.

Think of some things you would like to do outdoors. Explain these ideas to your family. Listen carefully to the ideas other family members have.

Akela's OK for the Bear Trail	Date
OR Akela's OK for the Arrow Point Trail	Date

CUB SCOUT LEADER BALOO SAYS:
When you have done three of these requirements, have a parent or another adult sign here.

Akela's OK	Date	Recorded by the den leader

13 Saving Well, Spending Well

People can do a lot of things with money. They can buy or build a house. Cars, clothes, food—almost everything we need or use takes money. We can make some things. We can raise or grow some foods. When we do that we save money.

You might have an allowance, or you might earn money for the things you need each week. Money is going to be important to you all of your life. Now is a good time to learn how to manage it.

Do four requirements.

13a Go grocery shopping with a parent or other adult member of your family.

Compare the prices of different brands of the same item. Check the prices at different stores.

Read the ads in your newspaper.

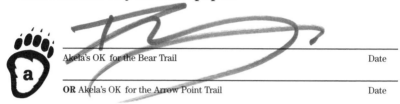

Akela's OK for the Bear Trail   Date

OR Akela's OK for the Arrow Point Trail   Date

13b Set up a savings account.

When you put your money in a bank or credit union, your money goes to work for you. The bank or credit union loans your money to people who need it, charging a fee (called *interest*) to the borrower for the use of your money. This interest is then added to your account. You may withdraw your money whenever you need it.

A savings account helps you save your money. The interest adds to the balance, and you may add more money as it becomes available to you. This makes it easier for you to save money for something special.

Akela's OK for the Bear Trail   Date

OR Akela's OK for the Arrow Point Trail   Date

REQUIREMENT

13c Keep a record of how you spend money for 2 weeks.

Date	How I Spent Money	How Much I Spent
_____	_____	_____
_____	_____	_____
_____	_____	_____
_____	_____	_____
_____	_____	_____
_____	_____	_____
_____	_____	_____
_____	_____	_____
_____	_____	_____
_____	_____	_____
_____	_____	_____

When you have finished the record, look over each line. Did you spend that money wisely? Did you buy some things you didn't need? What can you do to manage your money better from now on?

_____
Akela's OK for the Bear Trail   Date

_____
OR Akela's OK for the Arrow Point Trail   Date

13d Pretend you are shopping for a car for your family.

Look through car ads in the newspaper. Compare the prices of cars. Are the cars large enough for your family? How about miles per gallon? Pick one that you think is best for your family. Report your choice to your parent or guardian. Tell why you picked that car.

d

Akela's OK for the Bear Trail   Date

OR Akela's OK for the Arrow Point Trail   Date

13e Discuss family finances with a parent or guardian.

Find out how you can help with family finances.

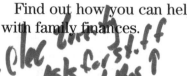

Akela's OK for the Bear Trail   Date

OR Akela's OK for the Arrow Point Trail   Date

13f Play a board game with your family that involves the use of play money.

Does the person who wins most of the time take fewer chances? Or more chances? Are you getting better at the game?

Akela's OK for the Bear Trail   Date

OR Akela's OK for the Arrow Point Trail   Date

REQUIREMENT

13g With an adult, figure out how much it costs for each person in your home to eat one meal.

Before the meal is prepared, jot down the cost of each of the foods used.

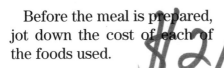

	WHEAT BREAD	ʰⁿ
	MILK ½ GAL	⁴⁵
	LETTUCE	⁷ᶜ
	CELERY	⁵⁷
	TOMATOES	
	ONIONS	
	BROCCOLI	
	CARROTS	⁵¹
	ICE CREAM	⁵¹
	POTATO CHIPS	³⁴
	APPLES	⁴⁵
	ORANGES	⁵⁷
	GRAPES	³⁴

Cost per meal

| People | Food cost |

Divide the total cost of the food by the number of people who will be eating the meal.

Is this more or less than what it would cost to eat out?

_____
Akela's OK for the Bear Trail   Date

_____
OR Akela's OK for the Arrow Point Trail   Date

CUB SCOUT LEADER BALOO SAYS: When you have done four requirements, have a parent or another adult sign here.

_____
Akela's OK   Date   Recorded by the den leader

14 Ride Right

Bicycle motocross (BMX), road bikes and mountain bikes, bike hikes—there are all kinds of bicycles and things to do with them today. Boys and girls and grown-ups, too, are riding bikes more and more.

Bicycling is fun, it's good for you, and it's interesting. But bicycling can be dangerous if you are not careful. Be sure you know the safety rules for bicycling, and be sure you and your family always keep your bikes in good shape.

The requirements to complete your Ride Right achievement are on the next page.

Do requirement a and three other requirements.

Rules for Bike Safety

1. Obey all traffic signs and signals.
2. Ride single file on streets and highways and keep to the right, with the flow of traffic.
3. Ride in a straight line. Don't do stunts or weave in and out of traffic.
4. Use proper hand signals when in traffic.

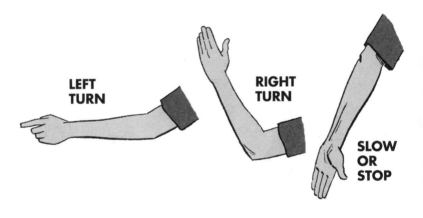

LEFT TURN

RIGHT TURN

SLOW OR STOP

5. Slow down and look carefully before you cross any intersection.
6. Be alert for other vehicles, especially for cars pulling out from the curb.
7. Don't shoot out of alleys and driveways.
8. Give pedestrians the right-of-way.
9. Don't carry another rider.
10. Don't hitch onto cars and trucks.
11. Be sure your bike has good brakes and a warning bell or horn.

12. If you must ride at night, be sure to wear light-colored clothing and to have a headlight on the front of your bike and a red reflector on the rear.
13. Always wear a helmet.

Akela's OK for the Bear Trail _____ Date _____

OR Akela's OK for the Arrow Point Trail _____ Date _____

 REQUIREMENT 14b Learn to ride a bike, if you haven't by now. Show that you can follow a winding course for 60 feet doing sharp left and right turns, a U-turn, and an emergency stop.

Note: Using a Snell- or ANSI-approved bike helmet is recommended.

Akela's OK for the Bear Trail _____ Date _____

OR Akela's OK for the Arrow Point Trail _____ Date _____

Keep your bike in good shape. Identify the parts of a bike that should be checked often.

_____ Brakes   _____ Seat   _____ Reflectors
_____ Spokes   _____ Chain   _____ Lights
_____ Pedals   _____ Tires

Which of these parts should be repaired by an expert only?

Explain and show how you protect your bike from bad weather. Always keep your bike under shelter when it is not in use. If it gets wet from rain or snow, wipe it dry. Keep the moving parts well lubricated. Have someone help you learn how to work with any parts that need adjusting.

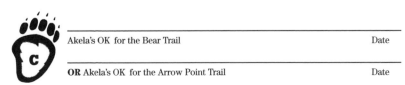

Akela's OK for the Bear Trail   Date

OR Akela's OK for the Arrow Point Trail   Date

14d Change a tire on a bicycle.

How to fix a puncture:

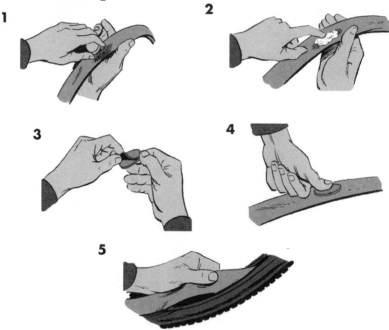

1. Scrape the tube over the hole.
2. Apply cement. Rub it in with your finger and let it dry.
3. Remove the cover from the patch.
4. Apply the patch with pressure.
5. Put a little air in the tube. Insert the tube into the tire and place it on the rim. Finish filling the tube with air. Check the air pressure.

Akela's OK for the Bear Trail   Date

OR Akela's OK for the Arrow Point Trail   Date

14e Protect your bike from theft. Use a bicycle lock.

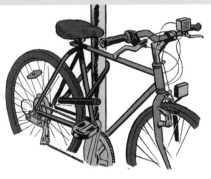

Write down your bicycle's serial number and keep it in a safe place. Have your name engraved somewhere on your bike.

Akela's OK for the Bear Trail   Date

OR Akela's OK for the Arrow Point Trail   Date

14f Ride a bike for 1 mile without rest. Be sure to obey all traffic rules.

Akela's OK for the Bear Trail   Date

OR Akela's OK for the Arrow Point Trail   Date

14g Plan and take a family bike hike.

Akela's OK for the Bear Trail   Date

OR Akela's OK for the Arrow Point Trail   Date

CUB SCOUT LEADER BALOO SAYS: When you have done requirement *a* and three other requirements, have a parent or another adult sign here.

_____   _____   _____
Akela's OK   Date   Recorded by the den leader

Let's play a game! Everybody likes games, especially outdoor games. Here are some game ideas. You might have played some of them, but you will probably find new ones. Games are fun and they teach you how to think before you act.

Do two requirements.

REQUIREMENT

15a Set up the equipment and play any two of these outdoor games with your family or friends.

————Backyard golf ————Kickball
————Badminton ————Softball
————Croquet ————Tetherball
————Sidewalk ————Horseshoes
shuffleboard ————Volleyball

NOTE for Akela: Ask your son's den leader to show you "Cub Scout Sports: Badminton," "Cub Scout Sports: Softball," and "Cub Scout Sports: Volleyball," in the *Cub Scout Academics and Sports Program Guide.*

Akela's OK for the Bear Trail _____ Date

OR Akela's OK for the Arrow Point Trail _____ Date

Achievement 15 127

15b Play two organized games with your den.

Pick games
that everyone
can play.

Akela's OK for the Bear Trail   Date

OR Akela's OK for the Arrow Point Trail   Date

REQUIREMENT 15c

Select a game that your den has never played. Explain the rules. Tell them how to play it, and then play it with them.

Did they understand your explanation? Do you think they will want to play it again?

Akela's OK for the Bear Trail _____ Date

OR Akela's OK for the Arrow Point Trail _____ Date

CUB SCOUT LEADER BALOO SAYS: When you have done two requirements, have a parent or another adult sign here.

Akela's OK _____ Date _____ Recorded by the den leader

Achievement 15   **129**

Building Muscles

Games, stunts, and contests with other Cub Scouts help you become physically fit and alert. Den and pack activities are aimed at keeping you healthy.

This achievement will develop your speed, balance, and reactions. The more you practice, the stronger you will become. A strong body is important to you now, and it will be even more important to you as you grow older.

Do all three requirements.

Do physical fitness stretching exercises. Then do curl-ups, push-ups, the standing long jump, and the softball throw.

Stretching exercises

Curl-ups

Standing long

Push-ups

Softball throw

Akela's OK for the Bear Trail	Date
OR Akela's OK for the Arrow Point Trail	Date

____ **ONE-PERSON PUSH OVER LINE.** Face your opponent. Grasp his shoulders. On the word "Go," try to push him across the line. Your goal line is 10 feet in front of you; your opponent's is 10 feet behind you. Only pushing is permitted.

____ **PULL OVER.** Indicate a circle on the ground, 15 or 20 feet across. Stand back-to-back, lean forward, place your hands on the floor. Now grab your opponent's right hand between your legs. On the signal "Go," try to pull your friend out of his half of the circle.

____ **ONE-PERSON PULL OVER LINE.** Face your friend 3 feet away from him. Grasp his wrists and try to pull him across the goal line 10 feet behind you. Only pulling is allowed.

____ **SEATED BACK-TO-BACK PUSH.** Sit back-to-back. Fold your arms across your chest. Using your feet on the floor, try to push your friend over a line. Don't push or butt with your head!

_____ **FOOT PUSH.** Sit facing your friend. Have the soles of your feet touching with your knees bent. Try to push your friend out of a circle or over a line. Feet must always be touching feet. Push on the floor with your hands.

_____ **ONE-LEGGED HAND WRESTLE.** Hold your left ankle with your left hand. Take your friend's right hand. On the word "Go," try to get him to let go of his foot or lose his balance.

_____ **STAND UP BACK-TO-BACK PUSH.** Stand back-to-back with your elbows linked. Try to push your friend across a line 10 feet away. Only pushing is allowed.

_____ **HAND WRESTLE.** Grasp your friend's right hand. Stand with the outside of your right foot braced against his. Spread your feet so that you are well balanced. On the signal "Go," try to throw your friend off balance. The first player to move a foot or touch the ground with a hand is the loser.

_____ **ELBOW WRESTLE.** Lie on your stomach, facing your friend (who is lying on his stomach). Place your right elbow on the floor and clasp your friend's right hand. Try to force his hand to the floor at the command "Go." Elbows must not leave the floor. Try it with left hands.

Akela's OK for the Bear Trail	Date

OR Akela's OK for the Arrow Point Trail	Date

16c Compete with your den or pack in the crab relay, gorilla relay, 30-yard dash, and kangaroo relay.

CRAB RELAY

30-YARD DASH

KANGAROO RELAY

GORILLA RELAY

_____
Akela's OK for the Bear Trail   Date

_____
OR Akela's OK for the Arrow Point Trail   Date

Note to parents: If a licensed physician certifies that the Cub Scout's physical condition for an indeterminable time doesn't permit him to do three of the requirements in this achievement, the Cubmaster and the pack committee may authorize substitution of any three Arrow Point electives.

CUB SCOUT LEADER BALOO SAYS: When you have done all three of these requirements, have a parent or another adult sign here.

_____
Akela's OK   Date   Recorded by the den leader

Information is a big word with a simple meaning. It means *facts*, and telling someone a fact is communication. We can also get information from newspapers, books, magazines, radio, TV, and computers.

As you complete this achievement, you might be surprised to find out all of the ways we can give and get information.

Do requirement a and three more requirements.

17a With an adult in your family, choose a TV show. Watch it together.

After the show, talk about it.
- What did you like?
- What did you learn?
- What didn't you like?
- What would you have changed?

Akela's OK for the Bear Trail   Date

OR Akela's OK for the Arrow Point Trail   Date

 17b Play a game of charades at your den meeting or with your family at home.

Charades is a guessing game. During the game, you give information without talking, and your friends guess what you mean. Each part of a word is acted out. Suppose the word is "football." You might point to your foot. When your team yells "foot," you could pretend to kick a ball. Don't use your voice at all during this game.

Akela's OK for the Bear Trail   Date

OR Akela's OK for the Arrow Point Trail   Date

17c Visit a newspaper office or a TV or radio station and talk to a news reporter.

- Where does the reporter get the news?
- How does the reporter put the story together?
- Where does the story go after the reporter finishes it?

Akela's OK for the Bear Trail	Date

OR Akela's OK for the Arrow Point Trail	Date

REQUIREMENT

17d Use a computer to get information. Write, spell-check, proofread, and print out a report on what you learned.

Most computers are used to store or get information. If you have a computer at home, ask a parent or other adult family member to show you some of the information that it can help you find.

Computers are a part of our daily lives. They are a source of information, games, messages, and fun.

Software companies have different programs with various formats. Be sure the one you are going to use will work with your brand of computer.

Pictures that appear on your computer screen are called *graphics*. They can be used to make story illustrations, games, certificates, and many other useful things.

Akela's OK for the Bear Trail	Date

OR Akela's OK for the Arrow Point Trail	Date

REQUIREMENT 17e Write a letter to a company that makes something you use. Use e-mail or the U.S. Postal Service.

Tell them what you like about their product. Ask them if they offer company tours, free samples, or catalogs.

Akela's OK for the Bear Trail   Date

OR Akela's OK for the Arrow Point Trail   Date

REQUIREMENT 17f Talk with a parent or other family member about how getting and giving facts fits into his or her job.

How do they get the facts they need?
- Does someone tell them directly, or over the phone?
- Do they read it on paper, in books, or from a computer screen?
- What do they do with the facts?
    - Do they pass the facts along to others?

Akela's OK for the Bear Trail   Date

OR Akela's OK for the Arrow Point Trail   Date

CUB SCOUT LEADER BALOO SAYS:
When you have done requirement *a* and three others, have a parent or another adult sign here.

17

Akela's OK   Date   Recorded by the den leader

Achievement

18 Jot It Down

Writing is one of the most important things humankind has learned to do. Writing lets us send messages to faraway places, make a lasting record of things we want to remember, and read what others have done or thought in the past. Being able to write clearly is a useful and satisfying skill. Do this achievement to learn more about it.

Do requirement *h* and four other requirements.

18a Make a list of the things you want to do today. Check them off when you have done them.

Before you go to bed, make a list of the things you should do tomorrow. Put the list on the bulletin board or someplace where you will see it often so you won't forget anything.

Akela's OK for the Bear Trail _____ Date

OR Akela's OK for the Arrow Point Trail _____ Date

18b Write two letters to relatives or friends.

Tell them what you have been doing in Cub Scouting.

Akela's OK for the Bear Trail _____ Date

OR Akela's OK for the Arrow Point Trail _____ Date

18c Keep a daily record of your activities for 2 weeks.

Time yourself. When do you:　　　　　　　TIME

　　Get up in the morning?　　　　　　　_____

　　Eat breakfast?　　　　　　　　　　　_____

　　Go to school?　　　　　　　　　　　_____

　　Eat lunch?　　　　　　　　　　　　　_____

　　Get home from school?　　　　　　　_____

　　Eat supper?　　　　　　　　　　　　_____

　　Do homework?　　　　　　　　　　　_____

　　Watch TV?　　　　　　　　　　　　　_____

　　Go to bed?　　　　　　　　　　　　　_____

Time yourself like this for 3 or 4 days. For the rest of the days, write what you did in the mornings, afternoons, and evenings.

Akela's OK for the Bear Trail　　　　　　　　　　　　　　Date

_____

OR Akela's OK for the Arrow Point Trail　　　　　　　　　Date

18d Write an invitation to someone.

Do you know a boy who could be a Cub Scout? Invite him to your den meeting.

Has your teacher ever come to a pack meeting? Send your teacher an invitation to your next pack meeting. Make your teacher an honorary member of your den.

Do you know what RSVP on an invitation means? It stands for words in the French language that mean "Please reply."

Akela's OK for the Bear Trail	Date
OR Akela's OK for the Arrow Point Trail	Date

REQUIREMENT

 18e Write a thank-you note.

When someone gives you a present, it's time to write a thank-you note. There are other times, too, such as when someone invites you to eat dinner, to see a movie, or to go swimming with them.

A thank-you note is always appreciated.

Akela's OK for the Bear Trail	Date
OR Akela's OK for the Arrow Point Trail	Date

18f Write a story about something you have done with your family.

You can tell your story just the way it happened or you can pretend you have your own time machine. Set the controls to any time in history from the Stone Age to the Space Age. One story could be about meeting Robin Hood and Little John in Sherwood Forest.

_____
Akela's OK for the Bear Trail   Date

_____
OR Akela's OK for the Arrow Point Trail   Date

18g Write about the activities in your den.

Your pack might have its own newspaper, and its editor would like to have your story for the paper. If there isn't a pack paper, post your story on the bulletin board.

_____
Akela's OK for the Bear Trail   Date

_____
OR Akela's OK for the Arrow Point Trail   Date

18h **Complete the Character Connection for Honesty.**

know commit
cc
practice

Honesty

Know. Tell what made it difficult to be clear and accurate as you wrote details and kept records, and tell what could tempt you to write something that was not exactly true. Define honesty.

Commit. Tell why it is important to be honest and trustworthy with yourself and with others. Imagine you had reported something inaccurately and tell how you could set the record straight. Give reasons that honest reporting will earn the trust of others.

Practice. While doing the requirements for this achievement, be honest when you are writing about real events.

_____
Akela's OK for the Bear Trail   Date

_____
OR Akela's OK for the Arrow Point Trail   Date

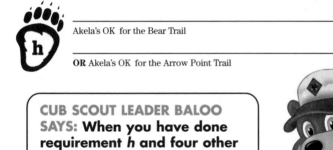

CUB SCOUT LEADER BALOO SAYS: When you have done requirement _h_ and four other requirements, have a parent or another adult sign here.

_____   _____   _____
Akela's OK   Date   Recorded by the den leader

Shavings and Chips

Your Cub Scout knife is an important tool. You can do many things with its blades. The cutting blade is the one you will use most of the time. With it you can make shavings and chips and carve all kinds of things.

You must be very careful and alert when you whittle or carve. Take good care of your knife. Always remember that a knife is a tool, not a toy. Use it with care so that you don't hurt yourself or ruin what you are carving.

Knives are usually used as tools, but they can be weapons, too. Many places, such as schools, prohibit knives. To be sure you never take a knife where they are banned, always keep your knife at home unless your parent or guardian and den leader tell you otherwise.

Do all four requirements.

REQUIREMENT

19a Know the safety rules for handling a knife.

Safety Rules

- A knife is a tool, not a toy.
- Know how to sharpen a knife. A sharp knife is safer because it is less likely to slip and cut you.
- Keep the blade clean.
- Never carry an open pocketknife.
- When you are not using your knife, close it and put it away.
- Keep your knife dry.
- When you are using the cutting blade, do not try to make big shavings or chips. Easy does it.
- Make a safety circle: Before you pick up your knife to use it, stretch your arm out and turn in a circle. If you can't touch anyone else, it is safe to use your knife.

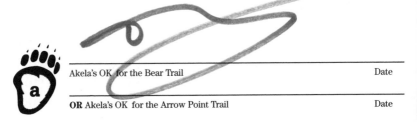

Akela's OK for the Bear Trail   Date

OR Akela's OK for the Arrow Point Trail   Date

19b Show that you know how to take care of and use a pocketknife.

SHARPENING A KNIFE. Lay the blade on a sharpening stone as though you were going to shave a thin sliver from the stone. Push the blade forward. Turn the blade over and shave the stone toward you. It is not necessary to push down hard. Continue this back-and-forth action until the edge is sharp along its whole length.

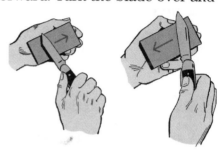

SHARPENING STICK

If you don't have a sharpening stone, you can use a sharpening stick. Look at the picture to see how to make one. Cover a piece of plywood with a piece of inner tube. Tack it down. Cover the inner tube with emery cloth and tack it down as shown.

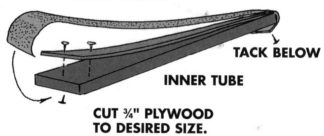

EMERY CLOTH

TACK BELOW

INNER TUBE

CUT ¾" PLYWOOD TO DESIRED SIZE.

SHAVINGS AND CHIPS

You don't have to be strong to whittle and carve, but you do have to be smart. Take it easy. Make a lot of small shavings and cuts. Here is the secret: Before you make a shaving cut, make a stop cut. At the place you want the shaving to stop, cut straight down with your knife. Press down and rock the blade back and forth until the cut is as deep as you want the shaving to go. Then make the shaving cut into it and lift away the shaving.

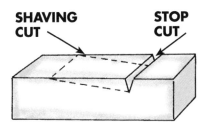

SHAVING CUT   STOP CUT

Akela's OK for the Bear Trail	Date

OR Akela's OK for the Arrow Point Trail   Date

 REQUIREMENT

19c Make a carving with a pocketknife. Work with your den leader or other adult when doing this.

TRACE THE PATTERN.

Eskimos carve beautiful animals from walrus ivory. They make seals, bears, dogs, and people. You can make a carving of a bear that looks like an Eskimo carving. Carve it out of soap.

FRONT AND BACK VIEWS

MAKE BOTH SIDES THE SAME.

Akela's OK for the Bear Trail _____ Date

OR Akela's OK for the Arrow Point Trail _____ Date

REQUIREMENT

 19d **Earn the Whittling Chip card.**

To earn the Whittling Chip you will need to read, understand, and promise to abide by the Knives Are Not Toys guidelines and the Pocketknife Pledge.

Whittling Chip

This certifies that

_____ has demonstrated knowledge of, and skill in, the use of a personal pocketknife. By completing these safety requirements and by promising to abide by the Knives Are Not Toys guidelines and the Pocketknife Pledge, he has earned the right to carry a pocketknife to designated Cub Scout functions.

Den Leader

Knives Are Not Toys

- Close the blade with the palm of your hand.
- Never use a knife on something that will dull or break it.
- Be careful that you do not cut yourself or any person nearby.
- Never use a knife to strip the bark from a tree.
- Do not carve your initials into anything that does not belong to you.

Pocketknife Pledge

In return for the privilege of carrying a pocketknife to designated Cub Scout functions, I agree to the following:

1. I will treat my pocketknife with the respect due a useful tool.
2. I will always close my pocketknife and put it away when not in use.
3. I will not use my pocketknife when it might injure someone near me.
4. I promise never to throw my pocketknife for any reason.
5. I will use my pocketknife in a safe manner at all times.

POCKETKNIFE PLEDGE

In return for the privilege of carrying a pocketknife to designated Cub Scout functions, I agree to the following:

1. I will treat my pocketknife with the respect due a useful tool.
2. I will always close my pocketknife and put it away when not in use.
3. I will not use my pocketknife when it might injure someone near me.
4. I promise never to throw my pocketknife for any reason.
5. I will use my pocketknife in a safe manner at all times.

_____
Signature

Akela's OK for the Bear Trail _____ Date

OR Akela's OK for the Arrow Point Trail _____ Date

CUB SCOUT LEADER BALOO SAYS: When you have done four of the requirements, have a parent or another adult sign here.

_____ Akela's OK _____ Date _____ Recorded by the den leader

20 Sawdust and Nails

When you can cut wood to the right length and fasten it together with nails, you're a handyman, but there are more tools than just a hammer and saw. You will need something to hold the wood in place while you work on it. Sometimes you will need to make a curved cut or put a hole through the wood.

A good way to learn how to use tools is to watch someone using them. When you need to make something with wood, ask your parent or another adult to show you how to use the tools safely.

NOTE to Akela: Boys are not allowed to use power tools on any Cub Scout project. If power tools must be used, you should do that part of these projects.

Do all three requirements.

20a Show how to use and take care of four of these tools.

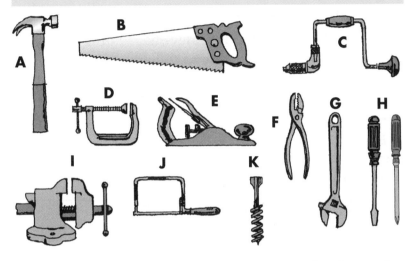

_____ **HAMMER (A).** Used for driving nails, for prying boards apart, and for pulling nails.

_____ **HAND SAW (B).** There are two kinds: one for cross-cutting, and another for ripping lengthwise along the grain of the wood.

_____ **HAND DRILL (C).** Uses drill bits to bore holes in wood and metal.

_____ **C-CLAMP (D).** Holds pieces of wood together after gluing.

_____ **WOOD PLANE (E).** Smooths rough boards.

_____ **PLIERS (F).** Slip-joint pliers have wide and normal jaw openings to grip things of different sizes. (Don't use pliers on nuts—use a crescent wrench instead.)

_____ **CRESCENT WRENCH (G).** This open-end wrench can be adjusted to fit many sizes of nuts.

_____ **SCREWDRIVER (H).** Sets screws.

_____ **BENCH VISE (I).** Holds wood in place for sawing or planing.

_____ **COPING SAW (J).** Lets you cut curves.

_____ **DRILL BIT (K).** Corkscrew-shaped drills are called drill bits. They are used to drill holes in wood.

Akela's OK for the Bear Trail   Date

OR Akela's OK for the Arrow Point Trail   Date

20b Build your own toolbox.

You will need five 1-by-6-inch pieces of wood. The two side pieces are 17½ inches long. The bottom piece is 16 inches long.

THE HANDLE IS A BROOMSTICK PIECE OR DOWEL.

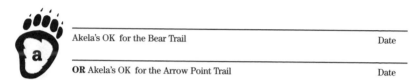

18"

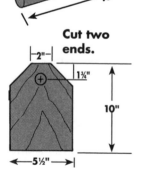

Cut two ends.

2"

1¾"

10"

5½"

The ends are made of the same 1-by-6-inch wood and are 10 inches long. Cut off the corners and drill a hole large enough for the broomstick piece. (The parts can also be cut from ¾-inch plywood.)

Did you know that wood sizes are measured when boards are still rough? When the rough edges are cut off, the board measures smaller. Your 1-by-6-inch board is really only ¾ inch thick and 5½ inches wide.

1" X 6" BOARDS

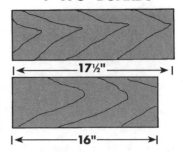

|←———— 17½" ————→|

|←———— 16" ————→|

Put your tool-box together with wood screws.

Cut two pieces 17½ inches long for the sides and one 16 inches long for the bottom.

Akela's OK for the Bear Trail _____ Date

OR Akela's OK for the Arrow Point Trail _____ Date

REQUIREMENT

20c **Use at least two tools listed in requirement *a* to fix something.**

Akela's OK for the Bear Trail _____ Date

OR Akela's OK for the Arrow Point Trail _____ Date

NOTE for Akela: It is best to use only simple hand tools and avoid power equipment when working with Cub Scout-age boys. Ask your son's den leader to show you Chapter 13, "Health and Safety," of the *Cub Scout Leader Book.*

CUB SCOUT LEADER BALOO SAYS:
When you have completed all three requirements, have a parent or another adult sign here.

20 _____ _____ _____
Akela's OK   Date   Recorded by the den leader

21 Build a Model

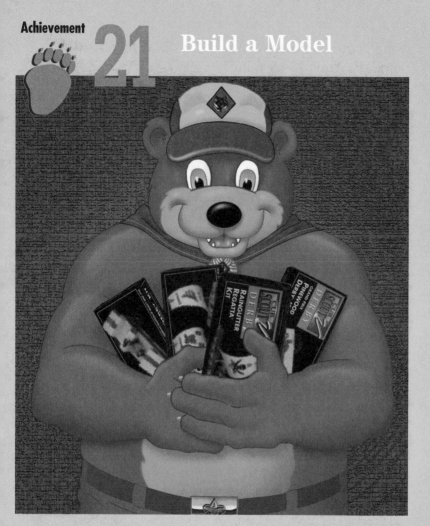

Model kits can be fun to put together. You can be proud of your model when it is finished. Most boys like to build models. Did you know that you might still be building models when you grow up?

Many grown-ups like to build models as a hobby. They build ships out of wood or large model train layouts they call *pikes*.

Models are also used by companies for serious purposes. Automakers build small models of their new cars before they actually start making them. Companies that build airplanes do the same things. People who design and build shopping centers and other buildings often build models to see what the building will look like. Model building can be serious business for grown-ups. As you can see, model building can be more than just going to the hobby shop and buying a kit.

Do requirement g and two other requirements.

 21a Build a model from a kit.

This can be any kind of model. Follow the directions, and feel free to change it any way you want to make it your own.

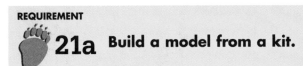

Akela's OK for the Bear Trail	Date
OR Akela's OK for the Arrow Point Trail	Date

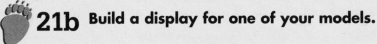 **21b Build a display for one of your models.**

If your model is a boat, mold soft clay into "waves" around the boat up to the water line. Remove the boat. After the clay has hardened, paint it blue and white to make it look like water with waves and whitecaps.

If your model is a race car, draw a short piece of the race track on paper or cardboard. Set up your crew in the "pits."

If your model is a dino-saur, give it a natural set-ting by using clay, leaves, and twigs.

_____
Akela's OK for the Bear Trail   Date

_____
OR Akela's OK for the Arrow Point Trail   Date

REQUIREMENT

 21c Pretend that you are planning to change the furniture layout in one of the rooms in your home.

Draw the outline of the room on a piece of paper. On another piece of paper draw the outlines of the furniture and cut them out. Draw your room and furniture cutouts to the scale of ½ inch = 1 foot. Use the paper cutouts on your room drawing to plan the changes. See how much easier it is to move your cutouts around than it is to move the fur-niture. Models let us see what the real thing will look like before it is made.

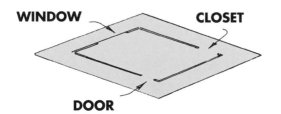

WINDOW   **CLOSET**

DOOR

  BED **CHAIR**

TABLE

Akela's OK for the Bear Trail   Date

OR Akela's OK for the Arrow Point Trail   Date

REQUIREMENT

 21d   **Make a model of a mountain, a meadow, a canyon, or a river.**

Use dirt, sand, stones, sticks, twigs, and grass cuttings.

Akela's OK for the Bear Trail   Date

OR Akela's OK for the Arrow Point Trail   Date

REQUIREMENT

 21e   **Go and see a model of a shopping center or new building that is on display somewhere.**

That model might have been built to help plan the construction. It might also have been used to show the project to community leaders.

Akela's OK for the Bear Trail   Date

OR Akela's OK for the Arrow Point Trail   Date

21f Make a model of a rocket, boat, car, or plane.

Use whatever you want to make it.

Akela's OK for the Bear Trail   Date

OR Akela's OK for the Arrow Point Trail   Date

21g Complete the Character Connection for Resourcefulness.

practice

Resourcefulness

Know. Review the requirements for this achievement and list the resources you would need to complete them. Then list the materials you could substitute for items that you do not already have. Tell what it means to be resourceful.

Commit. After you complete the requirements for this achievement, list any changes that would make the results better if you did these projects again. Tell why it is important to consider all available resources for a project.

Practice. While you complete the requirements for this achievement, make notes on which materials worked well in your projects and why.

Akela's OK for the Bear Trail   Date

OR Akela's OK for the Arrow Point Trail   Date

CUB SCOUT LEADER BALOO SAYS: When you have done requirement g and two other requirements, have a parent or another adult sign here.

21

_____   _____ _____
Akela's OK   Date   Recorded by the den leader

22 Tying It All Up

Sailors, cowboys, and mountain climbers all use good strong rope. Their lives sometimes depend on their ropes and the knots that hold them in place.

Do five requirements.

22a Whip the ends of a rope.

Ropes are made of twisted fibers. As long as the rope is in one piece, the fibers stay in place, but when the rope is cut, the fibers in the two ends begin to straighten out. Whip them in place with string or wrap them with tape.

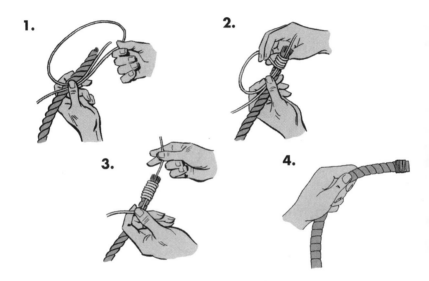

1.

2.

3.

4.

WHIP A ROPE.

Start with a 2-foot length of twine or cotton fishing line. Form it into a loop and place it at one end of the rope. Wrap the twine tightly around the rope, starting ¼ inch from the rope end. When the whipping is as wide as the rope is thick, pull out the ends hard and trim off the twine or fishing line.

Akela's OK for the Bear Trail	Date
OR Akela's OK for the Arrow Point Trail	Date

22b Tie a square knot, bowline, sheet bend, two half hitches, and slip knot. Tell how each knot is used.

SQUARE KNOT. A common knot made with two overhand knots. Square knots are used in first aid to tie bandages and to join two pieces of rope of the same thickness.

BOWLINE. A knot to make a nonslip loop at the end of a rope. It is a rescue knot when tied around the waist.

SHEET BEND. This knot looks like a bowline, but instead of making a loop, it joins ropes of different sizes.

TWO HALF HITCHES. This knot is used to tie a rope to a post, a tree, or a ring.

SLIP KNOT. This knot slips easily along the rope around which it is made. The knot itself is a simple overhand knot. It can be used to tie a rope to a post.

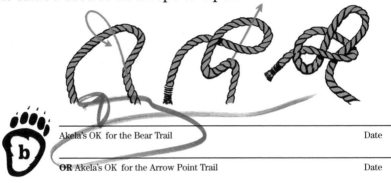

Akela's OK for the Bear Trail   Date

OR Akela's OK for the Arrow Point Trail   Date

22c Learn how to keep a rope from tangling.

Before you put a rope away, lay the rope out straight on a dry surface. Be sure there are no kinks or knots in it. Hold the end of the rope in one hand and coil the rope around your forearm from hand to elbow. Loop it around as many times as necessary to take up all of the rope. Take it off your elbow, hold the coil in your hand and take off the last loop with your other hand. Make a few turns around the coils with this end and pass it through the top of the coil held by your hand.

Akela's OK for the Bear Trail   Date

OR Akela's OK for the Arrow Point Trail   Date

22d Coil a rope. Throw it, hitting a 2-foot-square marker 20 feet away.

Put a weight on the end of your rope, heavy enough to carry your line out when you throw it.

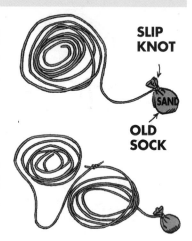

SLIP KNOT

OLD SOCK

Coil your rope in 1-foot loops. Hold half the loops and the weighted line in your throwing hand. Hold the other loops in your other hand.

Face the marker and swing the line toward it. Keep trying until you can hit the mark. It is important that you become good at this in case someday you need to rescue a person from drowning.

Akela's OK for the Bear Trail   Date

OR Akela's OK for the Arrow Point Trail   Date

22e Learn a magic rope trick.

Fold your arms across your chest, lean forward, and pick up one end of a rope in each hand. Unfold your arms and you have tied an overhand knot.

MAN OVERBOARD. Hold one end of a rope in your left hand with your thumb up. With your right hand thumb down, grasp the rope and turn your hand thumb up to match your left hand. Transfer the loop from your right hand to your left. Continue to make loops in this way until you get near the end of the rope. Then pass the end of the rope through all of the loops. Ask someone to pull the end of the rope while you hold the loops loosely in both hands. As the rope runs out, overhand knots will appear in a chain of knots.

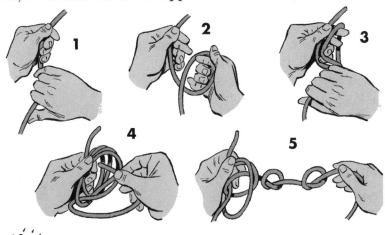

Akela's OK for the Bear Trail	Date
OR Akela's OK for the Arrow Point Trail	Date

22f   Make your own rope.

Use 24 feet of twine. Put the ends alongside each other and tie them in an overhand knot.

Soak the twine thoroughly before you start. Clamp a large nail in a bench vise and loop the knotted end of the twine over the nail.

Pull the twine loop out straight until you get to the end of the loop. Take the end of the loop back to the nail and place it over the nail and on top of the knotted end of the twine. Now pull back on the two loops to their ends.

Put the two loops on a hook that you have placed in a carpenter's drill brace. Using the brace and pulling back slightly to keep the twine tight, twist the four strands of twine together tightly until they choke up around the nail and the hook. Keep the twisting twine straight by pulling back on the brace.

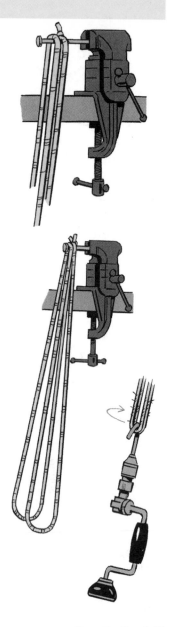

Place a chair or stool where you are standing and rest the brace on the seat. The weight of the brace will keep your new rope straight.

Now for the hard part: Let the rope dry for 24 hours. Then remove the nail and hook and whip each end.

With an adult's help, singe the loose fibers from the rope.

Akela's OK for the Bear Trail	Date

OR Akela's OK for the Arrow Point Trail	Date

CUB SCOUT LEADER BALOO SAYS:
When you have done five of the requirements, have a parent or another adult sign here.

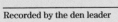

Akela's OK	Date	Recorded by the den leader

23 Sports, Sports, Sports!

Sports make for great times. They help us stay healthy and in good shape. They are fun to watch and fun to play.

Do all five requirements.

23a Learn the rules of and how to play three team sports.

Soccer

Basketball

Volleyball

Ultimate

Baseball or softball

NOTE for Akela: Ask your son's den leader to show you the pages in *Cub Scout Academics and Sports Program Guide* for each of the sports listed.

a

Akela's OK for the Bear Trail   Date

OR Akela's OK for the Arrow Point Trail   Date

23b Learn the rules of and how to play two sports in which only one person is on each side.

Tennis, bowling, marbles, table tennis, badminton, and golf are examples of individual sports.

NOTE for Akela: Ask your son's den leader to show you the pages in *Cub Scout Academics and Sports Program Guide* for each of the sports listed.

b

Akela's OK for the Bear Trail   Date

OR Akela's OK for the Arrow Point Trail   Date

23c Take part in one team and one individual sport.

Basketball

Team Sport

Tennibull

Individual Sport

Akela's OK for the Bear Trail   Date

OR Akela's OK for the Arrow Point Trail   Date

REQUIREMENT

23d Watch a sport on TV with a parent or some other adult member of your family.

Discuss the rules and how the game was played.

Akela's OK for the Bear Trail   Date

OR Akela's OK for the Arrow Point Trail   Date

REQUIREMENT

23e Attend a high school, college, or professional sporting event with your family or your den.

Did the players show good sportsmanship?

Did the spectators?

Akela's OK for the Bear Trail   Date

OR Akela's OK for the Arrow Point Trail   Date

CUB SCOUT LEADER BALOO SAYS:
When you have done five of the requirements, have a parent or another adult sign here.

Akela's OK   Date   Recorded by the den leader

Achievement 23   **173**

Achievement 24 · Be a Leader

Leadership means more than just telling others what to do. It means doing the right things. It also means listening to everyone's ideas before going ahead.

It's hard to be a good leader, but you feel good if you do your job well.

Your community and country need good leaders. In these requirements you will find some ways to be a good leader.

Do requirement f and two other requirements.

174   **Bear Trail • Self**

Help a boy join Cub Scouting or help a new Cub Scout through the Bobcat trail.

Do you know any boys your age who are not Cub Scouts? Being interested in others is the mark of a leader.

_____
Akela's OK for the Bear Trail   Date

_____
OR Akela's OK for the Arrow Point Trail   Date

Serve as a denner or assistant denner.

Denner_____   from _____   to _____

Assistant
Denner_____   from _____   to _____

NOTE for Akela: The denner is elected by the den for a short period, usually one or two months. Ask your son's den leader to show you "The Wolf and Bear Programs" in the *Cub Scout Leader Book* for more information.

_____
Akela's OK for the Bear Trail   Date

_____
OR Akela's OK for the Arrow Point Trail   Date

24c Plan and conduct a den activity with the approval of your den leader.

Den activity_____

Den leader's signature_____

Date_____

_____
Akela's OK for the Bear Trail   Date

_____
OR Akela's OK for the Arrow Point Trail   Date

24d Tell two people they have done a good job.

For example:
• A Cub Scout leads a good ceremony.

- A parent helps your den with an outing.

- A classmate does well on an assignment.

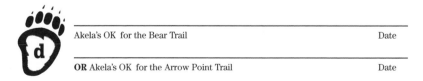

Akela's OK for the Bear Trail   Date

OR Akela's OK for the Arrow Point Trail   Date

Talk about these hard choices with a parent or another adult. What would you do if it were up to you?

- It is time to go home, but you are having a good time with your friends and they don't have to be home until 30 minutes later. What do you do?

- Your friends are going to ride their bikes to the other side of town, and they ask you to go with them. You know you are not allowed to do that. What do you say to them?

- A new boy has moved into the neighborhood. How do you become his friend?

- While your class is taking a test, the teacher leaves the room. Some of the students start trading test answers. Do you?

- What if another student asks you for an answer?

- Is it hard to keep from cheating?

Akela's OK for the Bear Trail   Date

OR Akela's OK for the Arrow Point Trail   Date

24f **Complete the Character Connection for Compassion.**

Compassion

Know. Tell why, as a leader, it is important to show kindness and concern for other people. List ways leaders show they care about the thoughts and feelings of others.

Commit. Tell why a good leader must consider the ideas, abilities, and feelings of others. Tell why it might be hard for a leader to protect another person's well-being. Tell ways you can be kind and compassionate.

Practice. While you complete the requirements for this achievement, find ways to be kind and considerate of others.

_____
Akela's OK for the Bear Trail   Date

_____
OR Akela's OK for the Arrow Point Trail   Date

CUB SCOUT LEADER BALOO SAYS: When you have done requirement f and two other requirements, have a parent or another adult sign here.

_____   _____
Akela's OK   Date   Recorded by the den leader

Now Follow My
Arrow Point
Trail

Now you are a Bear Cub Scout. Wait! You can still have lots of fun with this book. Baloo has *electives* for you, too. Electives are not like achievements. You may pick any requirement you like from the electives and do it. When you have completed 10 elective requirements, you have earned your first Arrow Point—a gold one. After earning a Gold Arrow Point, you may complete 10 more requirements to earn a Silver Arrow Point. Under your Bear badge, you may wear as many Silver Arrow Points as you earn.

When working on your Bear badge, you might have seen some achievements you wanted to try but didn't. Achievements that were not used to earn the Bear badge may be used as electives. However, note that unused parts of achievements that were used for the Bear badge may **not** be counted toward Arrow Points. These requirements now follow the same rules as the elective requirements. Each one is a separate project. You can mix requirements from electives and achievements that were not counted toward the Bear badge in any way to get the ten you need for each Arrow Point.

You may earn Arrow Points from the *Bear Handbook* until you join a Webelos den.

Remember these important rules: You may work on these electives all through your Bear year, but you cannot receive Arrow Points until you have earned your Bear badge. Unused parts of achievements that were used for the Bear badge may **not** be counted toward Arrow Points, but there are many more to choose from.

Space

What do you see when you look toward the sky? You might say, "In the daytime, I see the sun and clouds. At night, I see the moon and stars."

That's true, of course. You also are looking at our world's newest frontier.

Here's your chance to learn something about space.

Requirements

___ a. Identify two constellations and the North Star in the night sky.

___ b. Make a pinhole planetarium and show three constellations.

___ c. Visit a planetarium.

___ d. Build a model of a rocket or space satellite.

___ e. Read and talk about at least one man-made satellite and one natural one.

___ f. Find a picture of another planet in our solar system. Explain how it is different from Earth.

NO.	DATE	AKELA'S OK	✓ DEN CHART
1.			
1.			
1.			
1.			
1.			
1.			

CONSTELLATIONS AND THE NORTH STAR

Groups of stars have names. One star group looks like a W. Another one, the Big Dipper, looks like a big water dipper or saucepan. Two stars in the bowl of the Big Dipper point to the North Star. Make a pinhole planetarium with a tin can and a small nail. Punch tiny holes in the bottom of the can to mark each star's position in a constellation. Look through the hole in the top of the can while holding the bottom of the can toward a strong light.

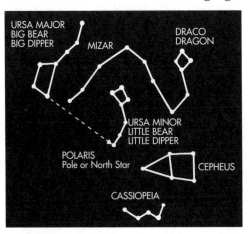

SATELLITES

Satellites are smaller objects that move around bigger ones. The moon is a satellite of Earth. Some of our TV and radio programs are brought to us by signals bounced off man-made satellites.

Everybody wants to know what the weather is and what it will be tomorrow. Will it rain out my team's baseball game? Do I need a jacket? Those are questions you have probably asked.

In this elective, you will learn how weather forecasts are made, how to measure rainfall and snowfall, and how to figure wind directions.

Requirements

___a. Learn how to read an outdoor thermometer. Put one outdoors and read it at the same time every day for two weeks. Keep a record of each day's temperature and a description of the weather each day (fair skies, rain, fog, snow, etc.).

___b. Build a weather vane. Record wind direction every day at the same hour for two weeks. Keep a record of the weather for each day.

___c. Make a rain gauge.

___d. Find out what a barometer is and how it works. Tell your den about it. Tell what relative humidity means.

___e. Learn to identify three different kinds of clouds. Estimate their heights.

___f. Watch the weather forecast on TV every day for two weeks. Describe three different symbols used on weather maps. Keep a record of how many times the weather forecast is correct.

This elective is also part of the Cub Scout World Conservation Award (see page 282).

NO.	DATE	AKELA'S OK	✓ DEN CHART
2.			
2.			
2.			
2.			
2.			
2.			

NOTE for Akela: Ask your son's den leader to show you "Cub Scout Academics: Weather" in the *Cub Scout Academics and Sports Program Guide.*

OUTDOOR THERMOMETER

For your outdoor thermometer, build a box with pieces of an old slatted shutter for the sides. This will keep the sun away from it but let air in.

Set it up facing north. It should be about 4 feet off the ground so the thermometer will be easy for you to see. Read the temperature at the same time every day. Mark it on a chart like the one shown below.

DATE	TEMPERATURE	WEATHER	WIND

WEATHER VANE

Weather forecasters describe the wind by the direction it is coming from—not the direction in which it is going. The notched end of your vane points toward the direction the wind is coming from. If you forget, look at the smoke, steam, or vapor from chimneys or smokestacks and you can see it blowing away from the wind. Toss up a few blades of grass and see which way they go. Check the wind direction at the same time that you check your temperature and rain gauges. Mark it on your chart.

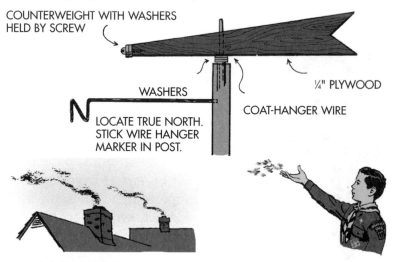

COUNTERWEIGHT WITH WASHERS HELD BY SCREW

WASHERS

LOCATE TRUE NORTH. STICK WIRE HANGER MARKER IN POST.

COAT-HANGER WIRE

¼" PLYWOOD

RAIN GAUGE

Use a large juice can (1 quart, 14 ounces). Set it on a platform with sides to keep it from blowing away. Choose an open place in your yard. Take your reading at the same time every day—morning, afternoon, or evening. If there is not enough water to measure in the can, pour it from the can into a measuring jar.

Snowfall can be measured by how much water it makes. Melt the snow collected and measure it in your measuring jar. One inch of water equals about 10 inches of snow.

CAN MUST
BE LEVEL.

BE SURE CAN
WON'T BLOW OFF.

CAN ABOUT 30"
ABOVE GROUND.

TO MAKE MEASURING
JAR, POUR 1" OF WATER
IN THE JUICE CAN. THEN
POUR IT IN A TALL OLIVE
JAR AND MARK 1". DIVIDE
INTO TENTHS.

You can measure snow on the ground by sticking a ruler or yardstick into several spots. Write each measurement down. Add them up and divide by the number of measurements. (Ask for help with this one.) This gives you the average depth of snow.

TYPES OF CLOUDS

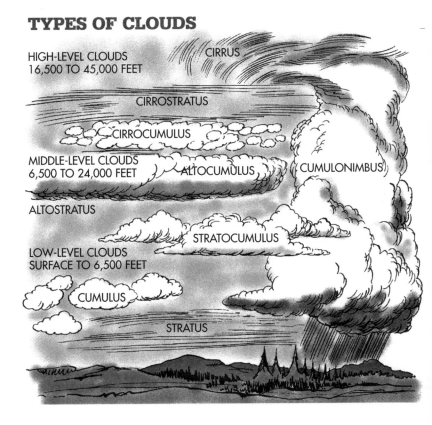

HIGH-LEVEL CLOUDS
16,500 TO 45,000 FEET

CIRRUS

CIRROSTRATUS

CIRROCUMULUS

MIDDLE-LEVEL CLOUDS
6,500 TO 24,000 FEET

ALTOCUMULUS

CUMULONIMBUS

ALTOSTRATUS

STRATOCUMULUS

LOW-LEVEL CLOUDS
SURFACE TO 6,500 FEET

CUMULUS

STRATUS

BAROMETER

Weather forecasters use a barometer to help predict whether it will rain or a nice day is coming. They can do this because the barometer measures air pressure.

Air pressure, or the weight of the air, helps them learn whether it will be fair or rainy. Warm air is lighter than cold air and is more likely to create a storm.

Early barometers were the mercury-in-a-tube kind. Modern barometers are smaller and easier to use, whether they are anaroid (with a dial) or digital. Air pressure can also be given in pounds per inch or in millibars. Average air pressure is less the higher you go, but at sea level it is 14.7 pounds per square inch.

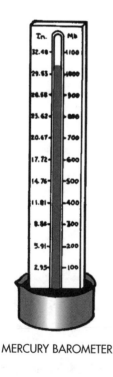

MERCURY BAROMETER

DIGITAL BAROMETER

ANEROID BAROMETER

RELATIVE HUMIDITY

Relative humidity is the term weather forecasters use for the amount of moisture in the air. If there is a lot of moisture in the air, the relative humidity will be a high figure, like 70 or 80. If the air is dry, it will be much lower, like 20 or 30.

On a summer day, if the temperature is 85° and the relative humidity is 80, you will feel hot and sticky. On a day when it's cooler, that much humidity won't bother you at all. It will be a pleasant day.

The weather forecaster finds the figure for relative humidity by comparing the amount of moisture actually in the air with the most moisture the air could hold at the same temperature.

Radio

You probably hear a radio every day without thinking much about it. Radio is just one of the things you have grown up with.

When radio first began, however, everyone thought it was wonderful that music and words could be sent all over the world without wires.

You can find out for yourself the excitement of the early days of radio and learn how a radio works by building one for yourself.

Requirements

___a. Build a crystal or diode radio. Check with your local craft or hobby shop or the nearest Scout shop that carries a crystal radio kit. It is all right to use a kit.

___b. Make and operate a battery-powered radio, following the directions with the kit.

NO.	DATE	AKELA'S OK	✓ DEN CHART
3.			
3.			

Many good kits are available for making crystal sets. This is the first kind of radio that was invented. Crystal radios get their power from the radio signal, so you will need a long, high antenna to make yours work. Even with a good antenna, there will be enough power only for a small earphone.

A transistor radio also can be built from a kit. This kind of radio gets its power from a battery, so it might be able to operate a loudspeaker. Ask an adult to help you. Follow directions carefully, and you'll have a thrill of "tuning in on the world."

Hang a map on the wall (one you have pasted onto cardboard) and keep track of all the stations you get.

Maybe you know someone who is an amateur radio operator or "ham." Ask to see his or her transmitter and receiver. Ask about some of the faraway places he or she has contacted by radio.

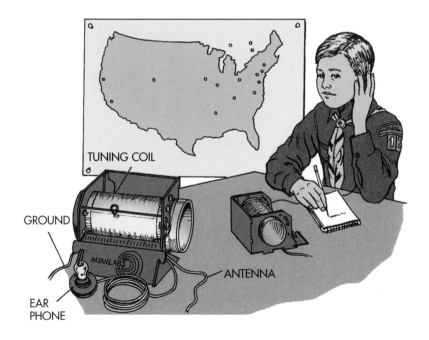

TUNING COIL

GROUND

ANTENNA

EAR
PHONE

Electricity

Wouldn't it be fun to make an electric motor that really works? Well, you can.

You can also make other things, like games and toys, that run on electricity.

As you build them, you will be learning about electricity—the power that runs so many things around your house and school and in your community.

Requirements

___a. Wire a buzzer or doorbell.

___b. Make an electric buzzer game.

___c. Make a simple bar or horseshoe electromagnet.

___d. Use a simple electric motor.

___e. Make a crane with an electromagnetic lift.

NO.	DATE	AKELA'S OK	✓ DEN CHART
4.			
4.			
4.			
4.			
4.			

Did your doorbell ever quit working? Sometimes when that happens, it's just because the connections are loose or the wires are corroded. If you know how to wire a doorbell, you will probably know how to fix it. You can mount a doorbell buzzer on a piece of wood to learn how to wire it. Get someone to work with you on this.

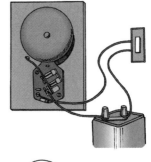

Electromagnets take some skill to make but are a lot of fun. You can make all kinds of tools and electric games with them. Get an adult to work with you on this.

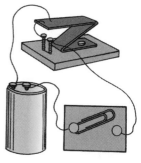

HORSESHOE
MAGNET

BAR
MAGNET

IRON OR STEEL
ROD

INSULATED
COPPER WIRE

Make up a separate sounding board. This can be used for many games. Make a question-and-answer board for your teacher. You can use it for many different quizzes. Write the questions and answers on sticky tape, and you can change them as often as you wish.

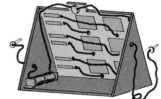

Any number of electric games can be made using a buzzer, a bell, or a flashlight bulb. A few basic types are shown. Now invent your own.

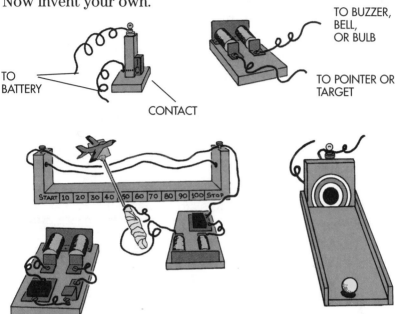

How to Make a Tin-Can Motor

Using the rotor pattern on page 195, cut five pieces of tin. Drill a center hole to fit snugly on a 2¼-inch finishing nail. Fasten the five pieces together with adhesive tape.

Wind magnet wire on the rotor until the space is nearly full. Leave 2-inch lengths of wire at the ends of the winding.

Wind ½-inch adhesive tape on the nail close to the rotor to form the commutator. Wind the tape until it is about ¼-inch thick. Cut two ½-by-¼-inch tin strips to mold around the adhesive tape, each covering about one-fourth of the surface. Scrape the wire ends of the winding and wrap each end around one of the tin strips. Fasten in place with ⅛-inch strips of adhesive tape.

Cut a 3¾-by-9-inch strip of tin, fold it five times to ¾ inch width, and hammer it flat. Bend it to the shape shown below to form the field bracket.

Wind several layers of wire around the top of the field, leaving a few inches of wire on each side for connections.

The brushes are made from strand wire wrapped around tin strips. Connect the field wire to the base. Fold tin strips to ½ inch width to form the uprights. Put a hole in each upright to support the nail. For power, connect to three dry cell batteries or a toy transformer.

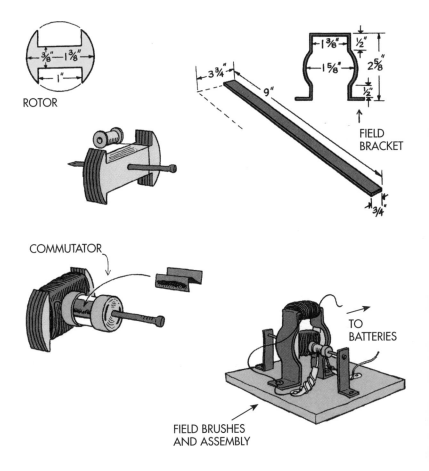

ROTOR

FIELD BRACKET

COMMUTATOR

TO BATTERIES

FIELD BRUSHES AND ASSEMBLY

5 Boats

Boating and sailing are great sports. Maybe you've already been sailing, but do you know how to rig a sailboat? Make a raft? Repair a dock? Do you know the safety rules for boating?

If your answers were no, find out now. Anchors aweigh!

Requirements

___a. Help an adult rig and sail a real boat. (Wear your PFD.)

___b. Help an adult repair a real boat or canoe.

___c. Know the flag signals for storm warnings.

___d. Help an adult repair a boat dock.

___e. With an adult on board, and both wearing PFDs, row a boat around a 100-yard course that has at least two turns. Demonstrate forward strokes, turns to both sides, and backstrokes.

NO.	DATE	AKELA'S OK	✓ DEN CHART
5.			
5.			
5.			
5.			
5.			

SAILBOATS

Sailing is a fine sport. Help an adult rig and sail a real boat—one you can ride in.

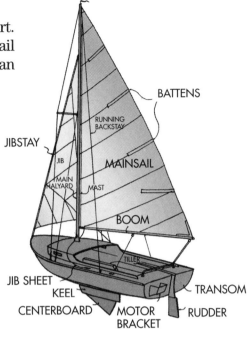

REPAIRING A DOCK

You get credit in this elective by helping your parent or any other adult fix up a boat dock. Check for boards that are loose, nails that are sticking up, or splintery wood that could cause an accident and injure someone.

CANOES

Repairing a boat or canoe is a good thing to be able to do. You'll be a proud Cub Scout if you're able to help a boat owner make repairs. Follow his or her instructions.

WOOD CANOE

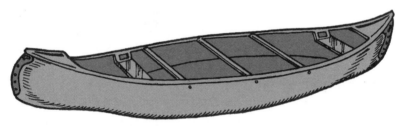

ALUMINUM CANOE

FIBERGLASS CANOE

STORM WARNINGS

The Weather Bureau uses a combination of flags and pennants to warn boaters of approaching storms.

Small-Craft Warning. One red flag by day and a red light above a white light at night.

SMALL CRAFT

Gale Warning. Two red pennants by day and a white light above a red light at night.

GALE

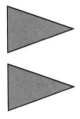

Whole-Gale Warning. A single square red flag with a black center by day and two red lights at night.

WHOLE GALE

Hurricane Warning. Two square red flags with black centers by day and a white light between two red lights at night.

HURRICANE

1. CATCH

ROWING

Grasp the oar handles firmly, knuckles up, wrists and arms straight, body bent forward.

Catch. Lower the oar blades edgewise into the water, not too deep.

2. PULL

Pull. Lean backward, pulling on the oars and bending your arms until your elbows come in against your ribs.

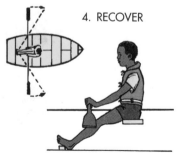

3. FEATHER

Feather. Lift the oar blades slightly out of the water and turn your knuckles up toward your face so that the blades are flat on the water's surface.

4. RECOVER

Recover. Bend forward and straighten your wrists and arms, ready to begin another stroke.

To do the backstroke, push on the oars instead of pulling.

To turn, pull on one oar while you hold the other in the water as a pivot or push it in the opposite direction.

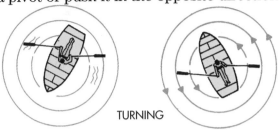

TURNING

Boating Safety Rules

- Know your boat—don't overload it. In a rowboat, one person per seat is a good rule.
- Put on a PFD before getting into the boat. Everyone should wear a PFD when in a boat less than 20 feet long. In some states, it's the law.
- Balance your load. Divide weight evenly from side to side and from bow (front) to stern (back).
- Step into the center of the boat when boarding or changing seats, and always keep low.
- If your boat tips over or fills with water, hang on. You can kick the boat to shore or drift in, but don't leave it. Let help come to you.
- Watch the weather. Head for shore if it begins to look bad. If you're caught on the water in bad weather, seat your passengers on the floor of the boat. Have everyone in the craft sit as low as possible. Head your boat into the waves.
- If you use a motor when boating with your family, use one that is appropriate for the boat. Too much power can damage your boat or even swamp it. Look on the boat for the capacity plate. It shows how many people the boat should hold and the recommended horsepower for the motor.
- Sharp turns are dangerous, so take it easy.
- Keep a lookout for other boaters and for swimmers.

6 Aircraft

Cub Scouts can learn a lot about airplanes and flying.

They can fly model airplanes. They can visit airports, talk to pilots, and be passengers in commercial airplanes.

There are lots of ways to have fun with airplanes and to learn more about them.

Requirements

___a. Identify five different kinds of aircraft, in flight if possible, or from models or photos.

___b. Ride in a commercial airplane.

___c. Explain how a hot-air balloon works.

___d. Build and fly a model airplane. (You may use a kit. Every time you do this differently, it counts as a completed project.)

___e. Sketch and label an airplane showing the direction of forces acting on it (lift, drag, and load.)

___f. Make a list of some of the things a helicopter can do that other kinds of aircraft can't. Draw or cut out a picture of a helicopter and label the parts.

___g. Build and display a scale model airplane. You may use a kit or build it from plans.

NO.	DATE	AKELA'S OK	✓ DEN CHART
6.			
6.			
6.			
6.			
6.			
6.			
6.			

HOT-AIR BALLOONS

The first successful flying machines were hot-air balloons. We fly them today for sport, but they still work the same way.

Air has weight, just like everything else made of matter. Air, and other gases, expand when they are heated. A plastic bag of hot air will weigh less than a plastic bag of cool air. The plastic bag of hot air will try to rise like a bubble in water because the cooler, heavier air around it tries to push in and occupy the same space. This is how a hot-air balloon works. Some balloons use other kinds of gas, such as helium, which is already lighter than air without being heated.

THERMALS

When the sun heats the ground, a layer of air near the surface is heated too and rises in a current of warm air called a *thermal*. In the same way, warm air from a fire rises up the chimney, drawing in fresh air for the fire and carrying the smoke away. Sailplane pilots find these invisible rising currents and ride them.

SAIL PLANE OR GLIDER

TYPES OF AIRCRAFT

TWIN-ENGINE AIRPLANE

COMMERCIAL JET AIRPLANE

HELICOPTER

A space shuttle flies like an airplane when it lands.

SPACE SHUTTLE

MODEL AIRPLANES

Many stores sell kits for making scale model airplanes that fly and solid models that don't. The kits have instructions for putting the parts together. After a little practice with these, you can design and build your own special model.

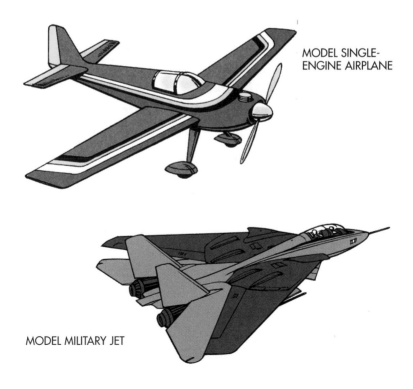

MODEL SINGLE-ENGINE AIRPLANE

MODEL MILITARY JET

Things That Go

Maybe when you were little, your folks got you a toy car to ride. It was lots of fun. Think how much fun it would be now to build your own! You can build it any way you like, and stop, go, or steer as you please.

On the next page you'll see plans for your Cubmobile. Try it and have fun.

Cubmobiles are not the only things that go. Have you ever seen a windmill or a waterwheel and wondered what they do? Here are plans for windmills and waterwheels that you can make. After you've made them, you might want to invent something of your own that goes.

Requirements

___a. With an adult's help, make a scooter or a Cubmobile. Know the safety rules.

___b. With an adult's help, make a windmill.

___c. With an adult's help, make a waterwheel.

___d. Make an invention of your own design that goes.

NOTE to Akela: Boys are not allowed to use power tools on any Cub Scout project. If power tools must be used, you should do that part of these projects.

No.	Date	Akela's OK	✓ Den Chart
7.			
7.			
7.			
7.			

CUBMOBILE. Use a helmet and safety belt.

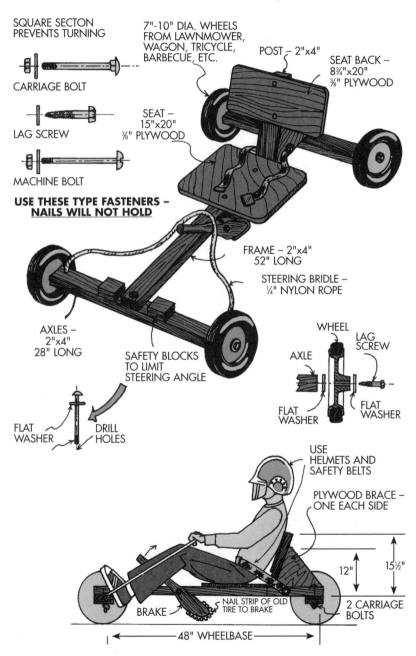

SQUARE SECTON PREVENTS TURNING

CARRIAGE BOLT

LAG SCREW

MACHINE BOLT

**USE THESE TYPE FASTENERS –
NAILS WILL NOT HOLD**

7"-10" DIA. WHEELS FROM LAWNMOWER, WAGON, TRICYCLE, BARBECUE, ETC.

POST – 2"x4"

SEAT BACK – 8¾"x20" ⅜" PLYWOOD

SEAT – 15"x20" ⅜" PLYWOOD

FRAME – 2"x4" 52" LONG

STEERING BRIDLE – ¼" NYLON ROPE

AXLES – 2"x4" 28" LONG

SAFETY BLOCKS TO LIMIT STEERING ANGLE

WHEEL

LAG SCREW

AXLE

FLAT WASHER

FLAT WASHER

FLAT WASHER

DRILL HOLES

USE HELMETS AND SAFETY BELTS

PLYWOOD BRACE – ONE EACH SIDE

12"

15½"

2 CARRIAGE BOLTS

BRAKE

NAIL STRIP OF OLD TIRE TO BRAKE

48" WHEELBASE

Sidewalk Safety Rules

- Pedestrians have the right-of-way.
- Watch out for cars coming out of driveways.
- Don't carry passengers.
- Don't ride in the street.

SCOOTER

WINDMILL

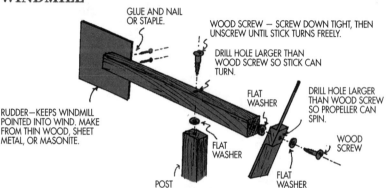

GLUE AND NAIL OR STAPLE.

WOOD SCREW — SCREW DOWN TIGHT, THEN UNSCREW UNTIL STICK TURNS FREELY.

DRILL HOLE LARGER THAN WOOD SCREW SO STICK CAN TURN.

DRILL HOLE LARGER THAN WOOD SCREW SO PROPELLER CAN SPIN.

FLAT WASHER

RUDDER—KEEPS WINDMILL POINTED INTO WIND. MAKE FROM THIN WOOD, SHEET METAL, OR MASONITE.

WOOD SCREW

FLAT WASHER

FLAT WASHER

POST

FLAT WASHER

PEOPLE HAVE USED WINDMILLS FOR THOUSANDS OF YEARS TO GRIND GRAIN AND PUMP WATER. TODAY WE ARE LEARNING TO USE THE WIND TO MAKE ELECTRIC POWER. WINDMILL BLADES MUST BE AT AN ANGLE TO THE DIRECTION OF THE WIND TO WORK. THE FASTER THE WIND BLOWS, THE FASTER YOUR WINDMILL WILL TURN.

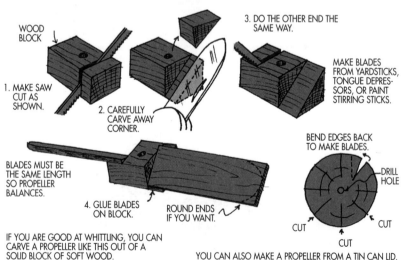

WOOD BLOCK

3. DO THE OTHER END THE SAME WAY.

1. MAKE SAW CUT AS SHOWN.

2. CAREFULLY CARVE AWAY CORNER.

MAKE BLADES FROM YARDSTICKS, TONGUE DEPRESSORS, OR PAINT STIRRING STICKS.

BLADES MUST BE THE SAME LENGTH SO PROPELLER BALANCES.

4. GLUE BLADES ON BLOCK.

ROUND ENDS IF YOU WANT.

BEND EDGES BACK TO MAKE BLADES.

DRILL HOLE

CUT   CUT

CUT

IF YOU ARE GOOD AT WHITTLING, YOU CAN CARVE A PROPELLER LIKE THIS OUT OF A SOLID BLOCK OF SOFT WOOD.

YOU CAN ALSO MAKE A PROPELLER FROM A TIN CAN LID. MAKE 8 CUTS WITH TIN SNIPS (WEAR HEAVY COTTON WORK GLOVES) AND BEND EDGES BACK TO MAKE BLADES.

WATERWHEEL

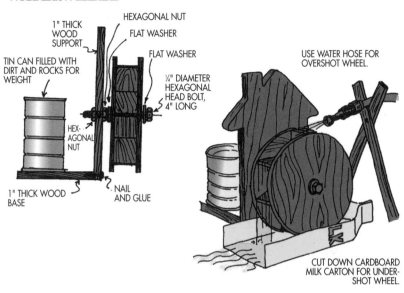

1" THICK WOOD SUPPORT

HEXAGONAL NUT

FLAT WASHER

FLAT WASHER

TIN CAN FILLED WITH DIRT AND ROCKS FOR WEIGHT

¼" DIAMETER HEXAGONAL HEAD BOLT, 4" LONG

HEX-AGONAL NUT

1" THICK WOOD BASE

NAIL AND GLUE

USE WATER HOSE FOR OVERSHOT WHEEL.

CUT DOWN CARDBOARD MILK CARTON FOR UNDER-SHOT WHEEL.

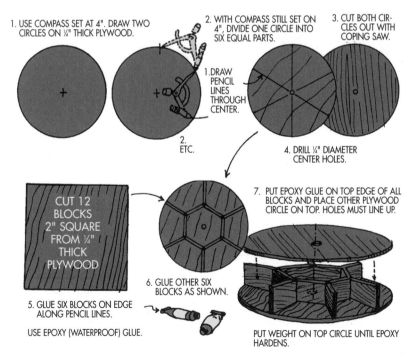

1. USE COMPASS SET AT 4". DRAW TWO CIRCLES ON ¼" THICK PLYWOOD.

2. WITH COMPASS STILL SET ON 4", DIVIDE ONE CIRCLE INTO SIX EQUAL PARTS.

3. CUT BOTH CIR-CLES OUT WITH COPING SAW.

1. DRAW PENCIL LINES THROUGH CENTER.

2. ETC.

4. DRILL ¼" DIAMETER CENTER HOLES.

CUT 12 BLOCKS 2" SQUARE FROM ¼" THICK PLYWOOD

7. PUT EPOXY GLUE ON TOP EDGE OF ALL BLOCKS AND PLACE OTHER PLYWOOD CIRCLE ON TOP. HOLES MUST LINE UP.

6. GLUE OTHER SIX BLOCKS AS SHOWN.

5. GLUE SIX BLOCKS ON EDGE ALONG PENCIL LINES.

USE EPOXY (WATERPROOF) GLUE.

PUT WEIGHT ON TOP CIRCLE UNTIL EPOXY HARDENS.

Cub Scout Band

Here comes the band—the Cub Scout band!

You can play music even if you have never had a lesson. You can even make your own instrument. Learn how in this elective.

Strike up the band!

Requirements

___a. Make and play a homemade musical instrument—cigar-box banjo, washtub bull fiddle, a drum or rhythm set, tambourine, etc.

___b. Learn to play two familiar tunes on any musical instrument.

___c. Play in a den band using homemade or regular musical instruments. Play at a pack meeting.

___d. Play two tunes on any recognized band or orchestra instrument.

NO.	DATE	AKELA'S OK	✓ DEN CHART
8.			
8.			
8.			
8.			
8.			

NOTE to Akela: Also see the pages on music in the *Cub Scout Academics and Sports Program Guide.*

All you need to get started is the desire to learn to play music. Try the simple instruments first until you find one you would like to play well. Then, practice!

If you are lucky enough to be studying with a music teacher, keep it up. Remember, you must practice to play well.

HOMEMADE MUSICAL INSTRUMENTS

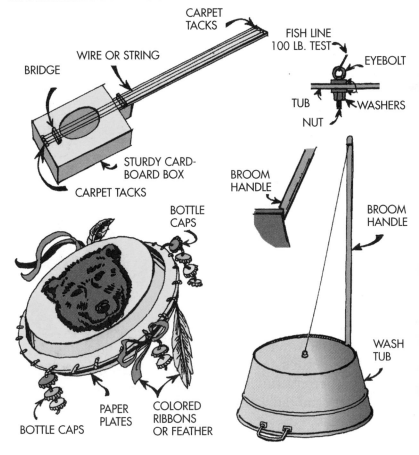

CARPET TACKS

FISH LINE 100 LB. TEST

EYEBOLT

WIRE OR STRING

BRIDGE

TUB

WASHERS

NUT

STURDY CARD-BOARD BOX

CARPET TACKS

BROOM HANDLE

BROOM HANDLE

BOTTLE CAPS

WASH TUB

BOTTLE CAPS

PAPER PLATES

COLORED RIBBONS OR FEATHER

STICKS, BONES, and BLOCKS. Use ½-inch and 1-inch dowels, 8 and 12 inches long. Notch some of them. Clean and dry short ribs of beef. Make hand-size sandpaper blocks.

RATTLES. Use gourds, spice boxes, small cans, shells, coconuts, paper tubes, or paper sacks for rattles. Put dried beans, peas, noodles, macaroni, sand, buttons, or beads in them.

TRIANGLES. Use a 12-inch-long brass pipe. Strike it with a 6-inch-long solid brass rod. Also use a horseshoe and spike and a pencil in a glass.

DRUMS. Use canvas, inner tube, or animal skin for drum heads. The drum body could be a tin can, ice-cream carton, cereal box, fiber drainpipe, or plastic pipe.

BOTTLE FLUTE. Place empty bottles on a tray in order of size. When you blow into the bottles, each one sounds different. Tune by adding water and adjusting the water levels.

Bottles are tuned, rubber bands are all in place, strings are tightened up, the washboard is handy—okay, strike up the band! Homemade bands are lots of fun. With a little practice you can get great music out of the simplest things.

Go to your library for more ideas or ask your music teacher for suggestions of instruments to make.

Art

Art is not just pictures. An artist's skill is used to make pictures and sculptures that tell a story and are pleasant to look at. That is what art is all about. Statues and stained glass windows are made for the same reasons. Study the art around you, and try your hand at making your own.

Requirements

___a. Do an original art project and show it at a pack meeting. Every project you do counts as one requirement. Here are some ideas for art projects:

Mobile or wire sculpture	Collage
Silhouette	Mosaic
Acrylic painting	Clay sculpture
Watercolor painting	Silk screen picture

___b. Visit an art museum or picture gallery with your den or family.

___c. Find a favorite outdoor location and draw or paint it.

NO.	DATE	AKELA'S OK	✓ DEN CHART
9.			
9.			
9.			
9.			
9.			
9.			

MOBILE

To make a mobile you will need:

- Three pieces of coat-hanger wire, different lengths
- Four cardboard shapes (any shape you like)
- Heavy thread or light fishing line
- Fisherman's swivel
- Pair of pliers
- Awl or nail for punching holes in cardboard

Step 1. Use the pliers to form a small loop in both ends of each piece of wire.

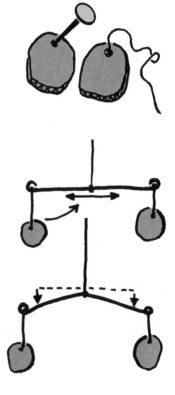

Step 2. Make one hole near the edge of each cardboard shape with the nail or awl. Tie a short piece of line to each cardboard piece.

Step 3. Tie one cardboard shape to each loop on the shortest piece of wire. Tie an 8-inch piece of line at the center.

Step 4. Slide the wire back and forth until it balances on the center line. Bend it at the balance point. This forms an angle that keeps the line from sliding back and forth.

Step 5. Tie this assembly to one end of the medium-length wire. Tie a cardboard shape to the other end. Tie an 8-inch line in the middle. Balance and bend the same way you did in step 4.

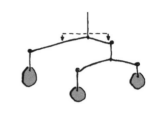

Step 6. Repeat step 5, using the longest wire and the assembly you made in step 5. Tie the hanging line to the fisherman's swivel. Use it to hang your mobile where it will be free to turn in air currents. The slightest breeze will make it turn and form ever-changing patterns.

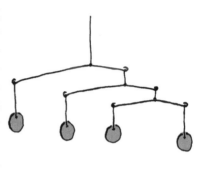

COLLAGE

A collage is a picture made up of bits of other pictures. The pieces are pasted down to make a new piece of art.

SILHOUETTE

Tape a piece of white paper to an easel or a door. Seat your subject between the paper and a bright light; his or her shadow will be cast onto the paper. Trace around the shadow with a pencil. Take the piece of paper down, lay it on a sheet  of black construction paper, and cut through both sheets along the pencil line you have traced. Paste the black silhouette cutout on a piece of white paper for display.

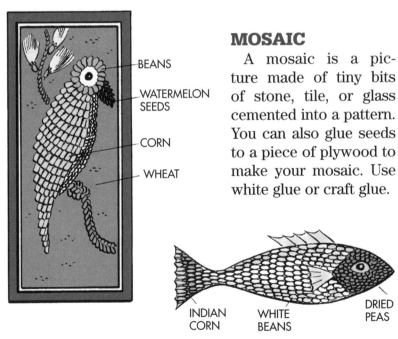

BEANS

WATERMELON SEEDS

CORN

WHEAT

MOSAIC

A mosaic is a picture made of tiny bits of stone, tile, or glass cemented into a pattern. You can also glue seeds to a piece of plywood to make your mosaic. Use white glue or craft glue.

INDIAN CORN

WHITE BEANS

DRIED PEAS

10 Masks

Since time began, we have been using masks in plays, games, and important religious ceremonies. We wear masks to pretend we are something besides ourselves. You might make a mask to wear one in a skit or play at a pack meeting.

Requirements

___a. Make a simple papier-mâché mask.

___b. Make an animal mask.

___c. Make a clown mask.

No.	Date	Akela's OK	✓ Den Chart
10.			
10.			
10.			

PAPIER-MÂCHÉ MASKS

The mask shown can be made on an oval dish. Turn the dish upside down and coat it lightly with shortening so the mask won't stick when you're through. Tear newspapers into strips. Make a paste with flour and water. Make it quite thick—about as thick as split pea soup. Now you are ready. Dip the paper strips into the paste mixture and lay them over the dish, overlapping and in different directions.

To build up the eyebrows, nose, lips, and cheeks, hold wads of newspaper in place and paste them down with long strips of paper.

After the mask is dry, paint the features. You can use a rubber ball for the clown's nose and rope, yarn, or brown straw for hair.

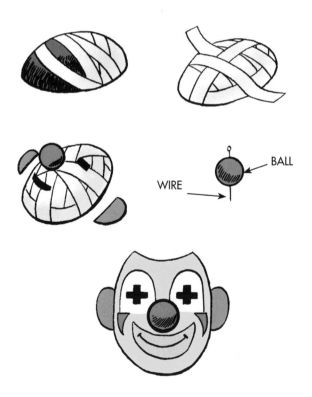

PAPER-BAG MASKS

Use a large grocery bag. Cut eye-holes and draw the face with a felt-tip pen. Cut another bag into strips. Curl the strips and glue them to the lion's head to make the lion's mane.

Glue two bags together to make a bull's head.

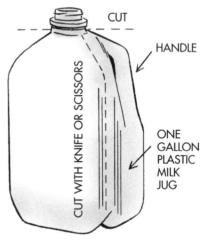

STYROFOAM OR CARDBOARD

GLUE TWO SACKS TOGETHER TO MAKE NOSE.

MILK JUG MASKS

Cut the milk jug in two with a knife or scissors. Trim off the top where the cap screws on. Each half can be used top- or bottom-side up to give you different face shapes.

The handle side (handle up) can be used for a knight's helmet, or for an "iron mask," sprayed with metallic paint. Remove a portion or all of

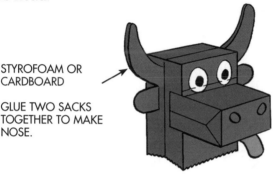

CUT

HANDLE

CUT WITH KNIFE OR SCISSORS

ONE GALLON PLASTIC MILK JUG

the handle, add cardboard ears, and you have a dog, bear, or other animal. Turn it over and paint it gold—it looks like an Egyptian pharaoh with a high forehead and ornamental head covering. Paint it orange; add black stripes, pointed ears, a cardboard nose, and presto! A tiger. Painted black with broom-straw whiskers, a "purr-fectly" terrific cat appears.

PHARAOH

TIGER

MOUSE

The other half can be used to make an owl, bird, or space creature. Make a knight or a clown, or paint it green to make a Martian. Many other characters can be made from this half.

Cut out eyeholes and mouth shapes with a knife or model-building knife. Glue on construction paper or felt decorations. Use your imagination; glue on bits of Styrofoam, yarn, fake fur, toothpaste caps, toothpicks, soda straws, or whatever you can find.

BEAR

ELECTIVE

Photography

Taking pictures is a lot of fun, but it can be harder than you might think. You need to use a camera to learn the secrets of taking good pictures.

Requirements

___a. Practice holding a camera still in one position. Learn to push the shutter button without moving the camera. Do this without film in the camera until you have learned how. Look through the viewfinder and see what your picture will look like. Make sure that everything you want in your picture is in the frame of your viewfinder.

___b. Take five pictures of the same subject in different kinds of light.
   1. Subject in direct sun with direct light
   2. Subject in direct sun with side light
   3. Subject in direct sun with back light
   4. Subject in shade on a sunny day
   5. Subject on a cloudy day

___c. Put your pictures to use.
   1. Mount a picture on cardboard for display.
   2. Mount a picture on cardboard and give it to a friend.
   3. Make three pictures that show how something happened (tell a story) and write a one-sentence explanation for each.

___d. Take a picture in your house.
   1. With available light
   2. Using a flash attachment or photoflood (bright light)

No.	Date	Akela's OK	✓ Den Chart
11.			
11.			
11.			
11.			

IMPROVE YOUR PHOTOS BY CROPPING.

Crop (or trim) your pictures so they show only the main subjects. Crop out background that does not matter.

BEFORE CROPPING

AFTER CROPPING

The more pictures you take, the more you will notice that the ones you like best are the ones that tell a story. The subject is doing something besides posing. The action tells something about the subject.

Picture Hints

- Take the picture in bright light, if possible.
- Keep the camera steady.
- If your camera is not self-winding, wind the film right after you snap the picture.
- Remember that every good picture has a center of interest.
- Try to take the picture of your subject against a good background.
- Store negatives in transparent envelopes, not regular paper ones.

BACK LIGHT   SIDE LIGHT   DIRECT SUN

TOO FAR AWAY

DON'T TILT THE CAMERA

GOOD

BUSY BACKGROUND

GOOD CONTRAST

AGAINST A POST

ON A ROCK OR CHAIR

DIRECTION OF ACTION

BLUR

GOOD

NO ACTION

12 Nature Crafts

Nature is a fun world to get to know.

When you go on a hike with a group in the woods, watch for animal tracks. Look at the trees and see how many you can name. If you look carefully, you will see that the rocks are many shapes, sizes, and colors.

Requirements

___a. Make solar prints of three kinds of leaves.

___b. Make a display of eight different animal tracks with an eraser print.

___c. Collect, press, and label ten kinds of leaves.

___d. Build a waterscope and identify five types of water life.

___e. Collect eight kinds of plant seeds and label them.

___f. Collect, mount, and label ten kinds of rocks or minerals.

___g. Collect, mount, and label five kinds of shells.

___h. Build and use a bird caller.

This elective is also part of the Cub Scout World Conservation Award (see page 282).

No.	Date	Akela's OK	✓ Den Chart
12.			
12.			
12.			
12.			

12.			
12.			
12.			
12.			

SOLAR PRINTS

You can buy special light-sensitive paper at hobby shops or nature centers, or you could use dark construction paper. Collect fallen leaves and arrange them on a piece of glass or clear plastic. Cover the leaves with the light-sensitive paper (coated side down) or construction paper. Cover the leaves with cardboard and use clothespins or clamps to hold it all together. Keeping the glass side down, find a sunny place, then turn the glass side up. If using the light-sensitive paper, expose the paper to sunlight for about five minutes, then remove the objects and place paper in water to "fix" the image. Leave the dark construction paper in the sun all day. If the paper hasn't faded enough on the first day, leave in the sun for another day.

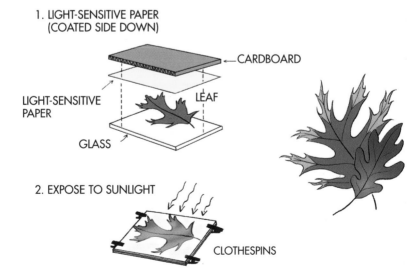

1. LIGHT-SENSITIVE PAPER
(COATED SIDE DOWN)

←CARDBOARD

LIGHT-SENSITIVE PAPER

LEAF

GLASS

2. EXPOSE TO SUNLIGHT

CLOTHESPINS

ERASER PRINTS

Use a stamp pad and a pencil eraser to print animal tracks. Study the animal tracks you find in the sand and mud along streams and mud puddles.

SHELL AND ROCK COLLECTIONS

Keep your collection in empty egg cartons. This will protect the shells from breakage. It will keep rocks from scratching shelves or furniture. Label each item.

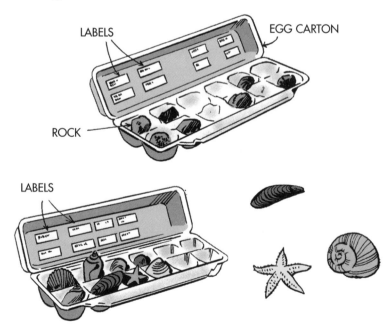

LABELS

EGG CARTON

ROCK

LABELS

WATERSCOPE

A waterscope will allow you to see water life more clearly. All you need are some cans, a plastic or glass jar, some wire, and some waterproof tape. Note five different examples of water life you see when using your new waterscope in a small stream or pond. Make sure an adult is with you.

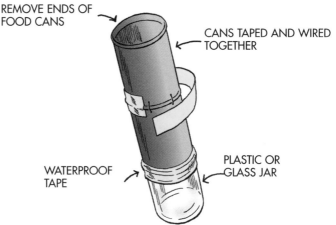

REMOVE ENDS OF FOOD CANS

CANS TAPED AND WIRED TOGETHER

WATERPROOF TAPE

PLASTIC OR GLASS JAR

BIRD CALLER

A bird caller requires a piece of hardwood about 2 inches long and 1 inch square. Obtain a screw eye. In one end of the wood, drill a hole slightly smaller than the threads of the screw. Turn the screw eye into the wood, take it out, and put some powdered resin in the hole. When the screw eye is turned back and forth, it will make a squeaky sound that attracts birds.

13 Magic

Now you see it—now you don't. Magic is a world of illusions and surprises. You can have fun with magic tricks.

Requirements

___a. Learn and show three magic tricks.

___b. With your den, put on a magic show for someone else.

___c. Learn and show four puzzles.

___d. Learn and show three rope tricks.

No.	Date	Akela's OK	✓ Den Chart
13.			
13.			
13.			
13.			

Look in your *Boys' Life* magazines and *Cub Scout Magic* for more magic tricks.

STRING THE WASHERS

Knot one washer onto the center of a string as shown. Next, raise the two ends of the string and drop the rest of the washers on so that they fall onto the knotted washer.

Separate the two ends of the string and hand them to a helper.

Place a handkerchief over the washers. Reach under the handkerchief and pull the loop down over the washer at the bottom to release the knot. Pull all the washers out.

The trick is in tying the knot.

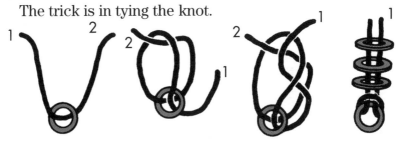

TRIANGLE TURNABOUT PUZZLE

Put ten checkers or ten coins on a table. Arrange them in a triangle pointing toward you. Don't put them close together (figure 1).

Tell the audience that the checkers or coins are flying saucers leaving their home bases. Say that they want to turn around and fly back home. Only three of them can fly in straight lines to make a new triangle pointing away from you.

Let the audience have plenty of time to try to do it. Remember, they can move only three items, and all must move in straight lines.

Show them how by making the moves shown in figures 2, 3, and 4.

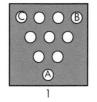

1

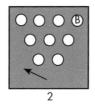

2

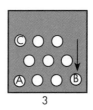

3

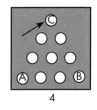

4

THE AMAZING HANDKERCHIEF

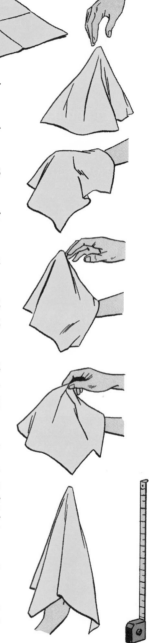

1. Spread a freshly ironed handkerchief on a table.

2. With your right hand, lift the center so that it stands by itself.

3. Lift it up to show that nothing is under it.

4. Spread the handkerchief over your left hand.

5. Lift it at the center; it stands on your hand.

6. Again, with your right hand, lift the handkerchief to show that nothing is supporting it.

7. Your left hand is concealing a mechanical tape measure, hidden by the back of your hand which is toward the audience.

8. Drape the handkerchief over your left hand. Turn your hand palm upward; grasp the end of the ruler through the handkerchief and pull out. The handkerchief will be standing in the air.

9. Push the center of the handkerchief down with the right hand. Pocket the handkerchief and metal tape measure with your left hand.

MAGIC DOLLAR

Say this as you fold and unfold a dollar bill: "If you had nothing to do, day in and day out, but look out of a dollar bill, you would probably think up something to do. George Washington likes to stand on his head. See?"

Hold up the bill to the audience with George Washington facing them, and follow these steps:

1. Fold the top half forward toward you (with George on the outside).

2. Fold the right half backward to the left.

3. Then fold the right half forward to the left.

4. Unfold the back half of the bill to the right.

5. Swing the front half of the bill to the left.

6. Bring the front portion of the bill upward, and old George is standing on his head.

How about that! (A new, stiff bill, or a carefully ironed old one, will make this trick easier.)

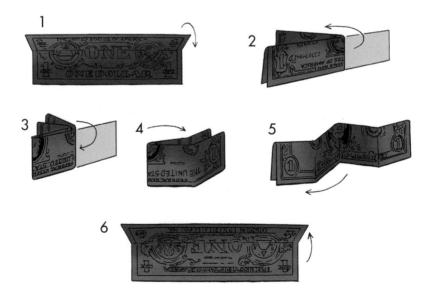

THE FLOATING BODY

Were you ever in a big crowd at a parade when you thought you saw a young boy who was taller than a grown-up? And then when you got closer you saw it was really a very small boy seated on his father's shoulders.

Well, that was an illusion. You thought you saw something strange, but it really wasn't.

Magicians use illusions all the time. One of the best is the floating body trick. With practice you can do it, too.

Here's what you need: a helper, a large bedsheet, a towel, two 3- or 4-foot-long sticks, and a pair of shoes and socks just like the helper is wearing.

Fasten the shoes and socks onto the sticks. Tie the sticks together. Roll a towel lengthwise and tie it onto the sticks to give them shape. They are supposed to be the helper's legs and should have some shape.

You will need a long, low bench that your helper can straddle. Place a cover over this so that it reaches the floor on the audience's side. The fake legs are on the floor on your side of the bench.

To perform the trick, follow these steps:

1. Have your helper seat himself on the bench with one leg on each side.
2. Hold the sheet to hide the bench from the audience.
3. The helper puts the false legs in place and lies backward on the bench.
4. Cover your helper with the sheet so that only his head and the fake feet stick out.
5. The helper places one hand on the bench and slowly stands up, holding his head far back, as if he were still lying down. He holds the sticks level with his other hand and raises them as he stands. This is startling if done slowly. It looks as if he is floating in air.

The trick looks hard, but with practice, the helper will be able to rise easily.

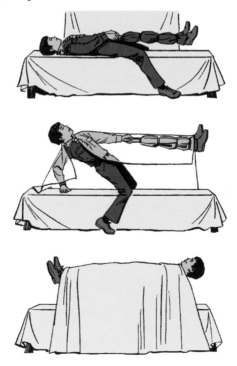

14 Landscaping

Some of our most useful plants are food plants. Other plants are grown for their beauty. Deciding which plants to use and how to arrange them is called *landscaping*.

Careful use of flowers, bushes, and trees can make our homes, neighborhoods, and parks nicer places to live and visit.

Requirements

___a. With an adult, help take care of your lawn or flower beds or help take care of the lawn or flower beds of a public building, school, or church. Seed bare spots. Get rid of weeds. Pick up litter. Agree ahead of time on what you will do.

___b. Make a sketch of a landscape plan for the area right around your home. Talk it over with a parent or den leader. Show which trees, shrubs, and flowers you could plant to make the area look better.

___c. Take part in a project with your family, den, or pack to make your neighborhood or community more beautiful. These might be having a cleanup party, painting, cleaning and painting trash barrels, and removing weeds. (Each time you do this differently, it counts as a completed project.)

___d. Build a greenhouse and grow twenty plants from seed. You can use a package of garden seeds or use beans, pumpkin seeds, or watermelon seeds.

No.	Date	Akela's OK	✓ Den Chart
14.			
14.			
14.			
14.			

YOUR FLOWER GARDEN

Make your flower bed interesting. Don't plant in rows but in groups as in this picture. Don't put all flowers of one kind or color in one spot. Putting light flowers in front of dark ones is the most pleasing. Plant small flowers like violets and pansies in front of taller ones like snapdragons and chrysanthemums.

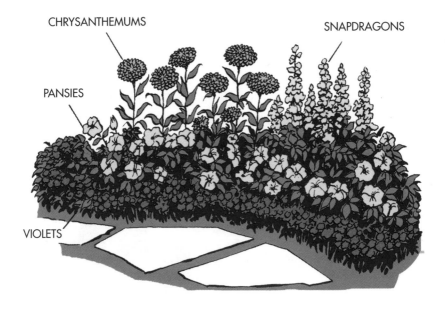

Plant your garden rows running as nearly north and south as possible so the plants can get lots of sun. If the ground is sloping, the rows should run crosswise, as shown. This is called *contour planting*. If the rows run uphill and downhill, rain will wash away the soil. That is called *erosion*.

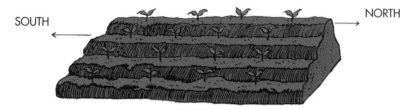

SOUTH

NORTH

BEAUTIFY YOUR NEIGHBORHOOD

Help plan for a small arrangement of bushes, shrubs, or flowers around the flagpole in your schoolyard.

Maybe planting a few shrubs along the block would help make the street where you live a more pleasant place.

Why not plant the kinds of things that attract birds? Here are a few:

Bushes—Barberry, bayberry, high-bush blueberry, elderberry, mulberry, common privet, staghorn sumac, viburnum, black haw, and yew

Trees—Box elder, birch, red cedar, flowering crab, dogwood, fir, hemlock, white pine, maple, mountain ash, wild cherry, and spruce

PLANTING SEEDS

Plant seeds in dirt or loose potting soil in a plastic bag. Add water until moist. Tie up and leave near a sunny window until the seeds sprout, then plant them in pots.

CLEAR PLASTIC BAG

SIMPLE GREENHOUSE

POTTING SOIL OR RICH DIRT

POTTING SOIL OR RICH DIRT

Start seeds in an egg carton. Put it in a miniature greenhouse.

MINIATURE GREENHOUSES

To make a simple greenhouse, cut out the sides and top of a cardboard box, leaving a sturdy frame. Place the seedling container in the bottom of the box. Cover the top and sides with plastic wrap, securing it to the box with tape. Poke a few holes in the plastic for ventilation, or leave a small area uncovered.

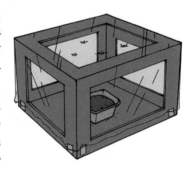

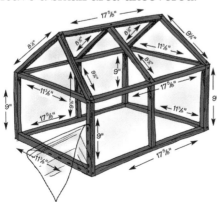

Make a greenhouse from ¾-inch wood strips. Use white glue and small box nails. Cover with heavy, clear plastic, using tacks or staples. This greenhouse fits over a cookie sheet.

Water and Soil Conservation

15

Every living thing depends on clean water and rich earth. It is important that we learn as soon as we can how to care for our water and soil.

Requirements

____a. Dig a hole or find an excavation project and describe the different layers of soil you see and feel. (Do not enter an excavation area alone or without permission.)

____b. Explore three different kinds of earth by conducting a soil experiment.

____c. Visit a burned-out forest or prairie area, or a slide area, with your den or your family. Talk to a soil and water conservation officer or forest ranger about how the area will be planted and cared for so that it will grow to be the way it was before the fire or slide.

____d. What is erosion? Find out the kinds of grasses, trees, or ground cover you should plant in your area to help limit erosion.

____e. As a den, visit a lake, stream, river, or ocean (whichever is nearest to where you live). Plan and do a den project to help clean up this important source of water. Name four kinds of water pollution.

This elective is also part of the Cub Scout World Conservation Award (see page 282).

NO.	DATE	AKELA'S OK	✓ DEN CHART
15.			
15.			
15.			
15.			
15.			

Soil is very important to you. Almost all your food and clothing comes from plants that grow in the soil and from animals that eat those plants.

Soil covers most of the earth's land and is made up of mineral and organic particles all mixed together by wind, water, and decay.

Soils are different around the country and around the world. Soil can be different colors, depending on how much decayed organic material is part of the earth (like leaves that have fallen from trees), how damp the soil is, or which minerals are in the soil (for instance, red soil has a lot of iron oxide in it).

Soils also feel different because some are made up of larger particles than others. For instance, sandy soil is made up of bigger particles than clay. You can feel the individual pieces of sand in a sandy soil.

Layers in soil are called *soil horizons*. These horizons exist because the way the soil is formed changes throughout the soil the deeper you go. The top layers, or topsoil, is made up mostly of decaying organic matter. We grow crops in the topsoil. Below the topsoil, you may find mineral particles mixed with organic matter. The deepest layers, which are not exposed to wind or much water, will be more like the original deep rocks that started the process of making soil a long time ago.

SOIL EXPERIMENT

Start with three cans the same size. Punch four holes in the bottom of each with a hammer and nail. Put clay in the first can, dirt in the second can, and sand in the third can. Fill all three cans half full. Pour a half can of water into each can, one at a time. Write down the time it takes the water to run through each kind of earth (until the dripping stops). The three kinds of earth are not good for growing things alone, but when mixed together they make very good soil.

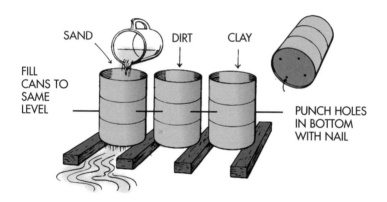

EROSION AND SOIL CONSERVATION

Soil is slowly worn away by rain, wind, and other natural forces. This is call *erosion*. But people have sometimes speeded up this natural process through activities such as building, mining, farming, and grazing.

Plants protect soil from wind and rain. Their roots hold the soil together. So clearing the land of its natural plants can be harmful to the soil and cause it to erode more quickly than new soil can be made. Sometimes, the eroded soil is deposited into lakes, streams, and rivers—polluting the water.

Soil conservationists work with farmers and other people to make sure that soil is used wisely and too much erosion is avoided. Farmers can add organic material to the soil or plow their fields in ways that prevent erosion. Ranchers can limit the amount of time their herds graze in one area.

KEEPING WATER CLEAN

Think of all the ways you use water every day (look back at your water-usage survey if you did achievement 6). You will see how important water is to you, so it is also important to make sure that it is clean and safe to use.

Water can be polluted from sewage disposal, waste chemicals from industry, and runoff of soil and pesticides from farmlands. Sometimes you will hear about oil spills that pollute the ocean and harm birds and other animals. Wastewater from homes can be a major source of pollution, although communities treat their wastewater in many ways to make it cleaner.

The U.S. Environmental Protection Agency has rules about the amount and kinds of pollutants that can be dumped into lakes and streams. People are paying more and more attention to the problem of water pollution. You can do this too by trying to limit the number of detergents, chemicals, or poisons your family puts down the drain in your home.

16 Farm Animals

You can learn more about farm animals even if you don't live on a farm or a ranch. If you do, it is easier, but if not, you can find pictures of different farm animals in magazines or on the Internet and learn how they are used. You can read a book about farm animals. Then when you go for a ride in the country, you will know what kinds of cattle, horses, pigs, and sheep you see.

Requirements

___a. Take care of a farm animal. Decide with your family the things you will do and how long you will do them.

___b. Name and describe six kinds of farm animals and tell their common uses.

___c. Read a book about farm animals and tell your den about it.

___d. With your family or den, visit a livestock exhibit at a county or state fair.

No.	Date	Akela's OK	✓ Den Chart
16.			
16.			
16.			
16.			

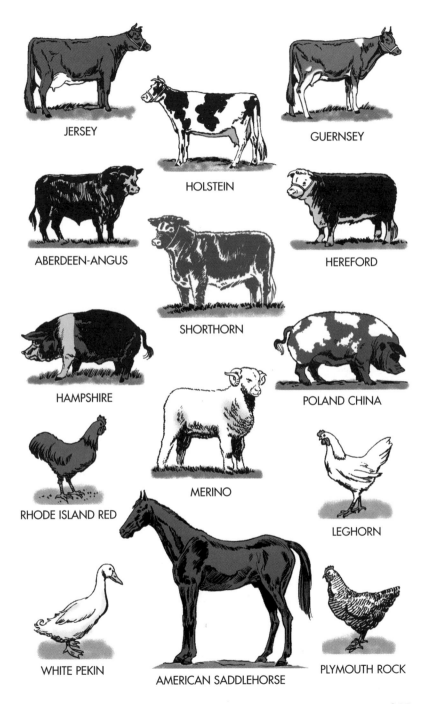

JERSEY

HOLSTEIN

GUERNSEY

ABERDEEN-ANGUS

SHORTHORN

HEREFORD

HAMPSHIRE

POLAND CHINA

RHODE ISLAND RED

MERINO

LEGHORN

WHITE PEKIN

AMERICAN SADDLEHORSE

PLYMOUTH ROCK

It seems as though there is always something that needs fixing around the home. Who takes care of these repairs where you live? Maybe you have already helped with repair work. If not, ask before you try. Talk it over. Make sure you understand what to do before you start. Electrical and plumbing jobs are not games. You have to know what you're doing or you could be hurt.

Requirements

___a. With the help of an adult, fix an electrical plug or appliance.

___b. Use glue or epoxy to repair something.

___c. Remove and clean a drain trap.

___d. Refinish or repaint something.

___e. Agree with an adult in your family on some repair job to be done and do it. (Each time you do this differently, it counts as a completed project.)

NO.	DATE	AKELA'S OK	✓ DEN CHART
17.			
17.			
17.			
17.			
17.			

FIXING AN ELECTRICAL PLUG OR APPLIANCE

With the help of an adult who is familiar with electricity, you can make repairs on light switches, sockets, and plugs. Be sure the cord is disconnected or the power is off before you start your work.

Also be sure that your hands and the floor are dry before you touch anything electrical.

SCREW-CONNECTOR PLUG

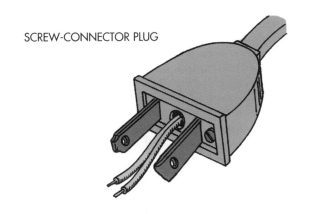

LIGHT SOCKET

HOW TO CLEAN A DRAIN TRAP

A drain trap is a J-shaped piece of pipe in a sink drain that gives a low spot to hold water. This keeps gas from the sewer from coming into the house. Sometimes it clogs up and must be taken off and cleaned out.

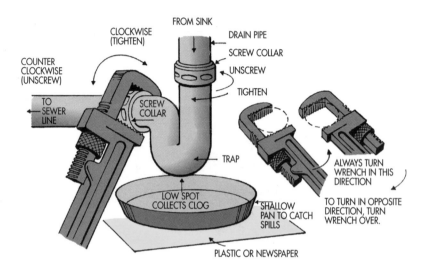

To clean a trap, first put down plastic sheeting or newspaper below the trap. The trap is full of water, so protect the area beneath the sink from spills. Use a pan to catch any drips.

Use a large pipe wrench to loosen the two screw collars that hold the trap. They have right-hand threads, which means that you turn them clockwise (the direction a clock's hands move) to tighten them. You will need to turn them the other way (counterclockwise) to unscrew them. They might be tight to start with, so you will need help from an adult with this job. After each collar has been unscrewed two or three turns with the pipe wrench, you can probably continue by hand. Be careful; the trap is full of water, soap scum, and other trapped things that you won't want to spill.

Unscrew the collars with one hand while holding the trap in the other hand so it won't fall off when the last collar lets go of it. When both collars are completely loosened, you can lift out the trap.

Carefully place the trap in the pan so it won't spill. Carry it to where you can dump it, but first remove the rubber seals. If they show signs of corrosion, you will need to replace them with new ones. The water can be poured into another drain, but the sludge and solid material should go in the trash. Flush out the trap outdoors with a hose.

Reverse the steps to replace the trap. Turn both collars at least two turns by hand to make sure the threads are matched up, and then make them as tight as you can with the pipe wrench. An adult should do the final tightening job to make the joints as leakproof as possible. Run some water in the sink to check for leaks. If you see any drips, tighten the screw collars more, or remove the trap and replace the rubber seals before putting it back.

18 Backyard Gym

Have you ever visited a gym or health club? You can build your own gym in your backyard. If you don't have room, don't give up. Your den can build a gym set to use in a pack outdoor-fun day. Here are some ideas. You can find more in *Boys' Life* magazine.

Requirements

___a. Build and use an outdoor gym with at least three items from this list:
   1. Balance board
   2. Trapeze
   3. Tire walk
   4. Tire swing
   5. Tetherball
   6. Climbing rope
   7. Running long jump area

___b. Build three outdoor toss games.

___c. Plan an outdoor game or gym day with your den. (This can be a part of a pack activity.) Put your plans on paper.

___d. Hold an open house for your backyard gym.

No.	Date	Akela's OK	✓ Den Chart
18.			
18.			
18.			
18.			

TOSSBOARD CLOWN

On any old plank or board, paint a large clown. Cut openings for the mouth and pockets. Make them different sizes. Nail or screw a brace to the back at an angle so your clown will stand up. Toss beanbags or balls through the openings.

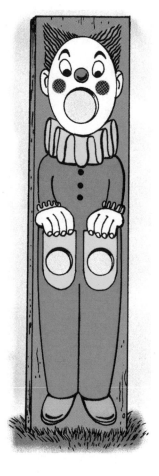

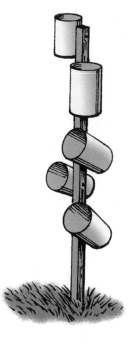

CAN CATCHER

Fasten large cans on a post. Aim some straight up and some slanting up a little. Try tossing a ball into each one. Try it from different places. This helps improve your ability to judge distance.

BOX GOLF

BOX GOLF

Set up nine cartons and number them. Throw your ball into carton 1. If you miss, throw again from where you pick up your ball. When you have gotten the ball into carton 1, throw to carton 2. Get someone to play with you.

Note for Akela: Check the tires to make sure no pieces of wire are sticking up through the surface.

TIRE WALK

TETHERBALL

BURY PIPE IN GROUND TO HOLD TETHERBALL POLE.

BACKYARD GYM

TRAPEEZE

WHEN YOU'RE FINISHED, I'D LIKE TO USE THE ROPE TO MAKE A TIRE SWING.

CLIMBING ROPE

BALANCE BOARD

RUNNING LONG JUMP AREA

Swimming

19

Swimming is a lot of fun!

When you learn to swim, you have a skill you can enjoy all your life. Whether you swim for fun or for sport, you can enjoy it winter or summer and share the fun with your friends. (Remember, **never swim alone!**)

> There is something about this elective that is different from any other. That is this rule: Whenever you are working on the Swimming elective, you must have an adult with you who can swim.

Requirements

___a. Jump feetfirst into water over your head, swim 25 feet on the surface, stop, turn sharply, and swim back.

___b. Swim on your back, using the elementary backstroke, for 30 feet.

___c. Rest by floating on your back, using as little motion as possible, for at least 1 minute.

___d. Tell what is meant by the buddy system. Know the basic rules of safe swimming.

___e. Do a racing dive from the edge of a pool and swim 60 feet, using a racing stroke. (You might need to make a turn.)

NOTE for Akela: Ask your son's den leader to show you "Cub Scout Sports: Swimming" in the *Cub Scout Academics and Sports Program Guide.*

NO.	DATE	AKELA'S OK	✓ DEN CHART
19.			
19.			
19.			
19.			
19.			

FLOATING

Hold your breath. Bend down in the water and clasp your hands around your legs below the knees. Presto! You float like a cork! Stretch out your arms and legs and you will still float.

BACK FLOAT

Stretch your arms to the side and lie back in the water, letting your feet float. Hold a deep breath. The water will just cover your ears. Relax and breathe normally. This is a good way to rest in the water.

Basic Rules of Safe Swimming

1. Be physically fit.

2. Have a qualified adult present whenever you swim.

3. Swim in areas that have already been checked and have no deep holes, stumps, rocks, cans, or glass.

4. If you can't swim, don't go in water more than 3½ feet deep. If you can swim 50 feet, it's safe to go in water up to the top of your head. Go in deep water only if you are a good swimmer.

5. Swim with a buddy—someone to help you if you get into trouble, someone you can help if he needs it.

6. Obey the rules. Have a good time in the water and learn to swim a little better each time you go in.

BUDDY SYSTEM

The buddy system makes swimming safer. Every swimmer is paired with a buddy who can swim about as well as he can. Buddies stay within 10 feet of each other during the swim and check in and out of the swimming area together.

All swimmers are checked in the water about every 10 minutes. The adult in charge signals for a buddy check with a single blast of a whistle or the ring of a bell, calls "Buddies!," and counts slowly to ten while the buddies join and raise hands

and then remain still and silent. Guards check all areas, count the pairs, and compare the total with the number known to be in the water. Two blasts or bells is the signal to resume swimming.

At the end of the swim, a final buddy check is made and every swimmer is accounted for. Three blasts or bells is the signal for immediate checkout.

SIDESTROKE

This is a good stroke for swimming a long way because it is not very tiring.

Lie on your side in the water. Either side is okay. Your legs do what is called the scissors kick. Part them in the water as far as you can, and then bring them together as hard as you can.

At the same time, reach forward with your arm that is lowest in the water, and then pull it hard through the water back toward your body. Make a shorter stroke with your top arm as you are pulling the bottom arm back.

JUMP ENTRY

Jumping into the water feetfirst with your legs and arms spread out and forward is a safe way to enter strange waters. Don't dive if you don't know what the bottom is like. You could hurt your head or neck if the water is shallow or if there is a big rock near the surface.

If you are jumping from higher than 4 feet above the water, keep your feet together and your legs straight. Hold your nose with one hand as you jump.

RACING DIVE

In swimming races, you want to start fast and land in the water in a racing position. Stand with your feet slightly apart with the toes gripping the edge of the pool or dock. Crouch slightly with your arms back and your palms up.

On the signal, leap and swing your arms forward. You'll land in a swimming position.

RACING STROKE

This stroke is called the crawl. It is used for fast swims, but it can be tiring over long distances.

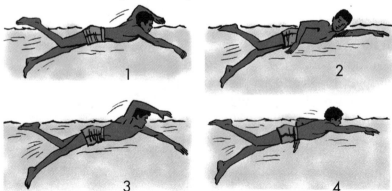

Start by floating facedown with your arms and legs extended. Begin to kick fast and evenly. Try to keep your legs straight.

As you kick, reach one arm forward as far as it will go. Then pull it back hard through the water. When it gets about half-way back, reach forward with the other arm and stroke.

To take a breath, turn your head to one side out of the water as you start to stroke with the arm on the opposite side.

ELEMENTARY BACKSTROKE

Begin by floating on your back, arms down at your sides. Bring your hands up over your chest to your shoulders. Reach straight outward and a little beyond your head. Then pull your arms back hard to your sides. At the same time you are beginning the arm movement, draw your knees out like a frog, keeping your feet together. Then spread your legs wide to the sides—just as you begin pulling your arm—and snap them together to the starting position. Breathe in through your mouth just before each stroke.

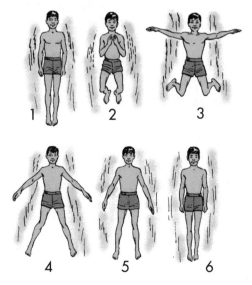

Sports

20

If you like sports, you aren't alone! Here are some more fun electives that will help you earn Arrow Points while you learn new sports skills. Archery and BB-gun shooting are restricted to day camps, Cub Scout/Webelos Scout resident camps, council-managed family camping programs, or to council activities where there are properly trained supervisors and all standards for BSA shooting sports are enforced.

Requirements

___a. In archery, know the safety rules and how to shoot correctly. Put six arrows into a 4-foot target from a distance of 15 feet. Make an arrow holder. (This can be done only at district/council day or resident or family camp.)

___b. In skiing, know the Skier's Safety and Courtesy Code. Demonstrate walking and kick turn, climbing with a side step or herringbone, a snowplow stop, a stem turn, four linked snowplow or stem turns, straight running in a downhill position or cross-country position, and how to recover from a fall.

___c. In ice skating, know the safety rules. From a standing start, skate forward 150 feet and come to a complete stop within 20 feet. Skate around a corner clockwise and counterclockwise without coasting. Show a turn from forward to backward. Skate backward 50 feet.

___d. In track, show how to make a sprint start. Run the 50-yard dash in 10 seconds or less. Show how to do the standing long jump, the running long jump, or the high jump. (Be sure to have a soft landing area.)

___e. In roller skating (with conventional or in-line skates), know the safety rules. From a standing start, skate forward 150 feet and come to a complete stop within 20 feet. Skate around a corner clockwise and counterclockwise without coasting and show a turn from forward to backward. Skate backward 50 feet. Wear the proper protective clothing.

___ f. Earn a new Cub Scout Sports pin. (Repeat three times with different sports to earn up to three Arrow Points.)

NO.	DATE	AKELA'S OK	✓ DEN CHART
20.			
20.			
20.			
20.			
20.			
20.			

HOW TO SHOOT WITH A BOW AND ARROW

Hold the bow level and lay an arrow across it, touching your forefinger. Nock the arrow with the cock feather

turned up. Face the target sideways. As you raise the bow to a straight-up shooting position, take aim and pull the drawstring back until your hand touches your chin. Keep your left arm stiff. Release the arrow smoothly by opening your string fingers quickly.

Archery Safety Rules

• Shoot only when a grown-up is with you.
• Never nock an arrow until you're ready to shoot.
• Never aim an arrow toward anyone; point arrows only downrange, toward the target.
• When not shooting, always point the arrow downward.
• Shoot only where you have a clear view all around.

The Skier's Safety and Courtesy Code

- Ski only when properly equipped and clothed.
- Never ski alone.
- Ski under control, which means being able to turn and stop when you want.
- Ski only on slopes suited to your ability.
- Try to check the trail before skiing down it.
- Respect the rights of other skiers.
- Keep yourself physically fit.

HERRINGBONE

SIDE STEP

NOTE for Akela: Ask your son's den leader to show you "Cub Scout Sports: Snow Ski and Board Sports" in the *Cub Scout Academics and Sports Program Guide.*

Ice Skating Safety Rules

- Always use sharp skates.
- Skate only on approved ice surfaces in places where skating is supervised by an adult.
- Never skate alone.
- Never skate or walk on thin ice.
- Watch where you are skating at all times.
- Never throw anything onto the ice.
- Never shove or grab another skater.

Four inches of new ice is a safe thickness for a crowd. Stay ashore until the ice is tested and approved for skating. Ice is unsafe after midwinter and spring thaws.

Springs bubbling up from lake or river bottoms will prevent water from freezing. Such openings in an ice field are known as "air holes." Streams, windswept lakes, tidal rivers, and salt water are slow to freeze and dangerous except after very cold weather.

Bushes, small trees, or danger signs should be used to mark unsafe spots in daytime. Flares or lights should be used to mark them at night.

RIME AND REASON

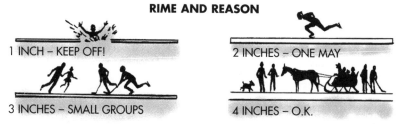

1 INCH – KEEP OFF!

2 INCHES – ONE MAY

3 INCHES – SMALL GROUPS

4 INCHES – O.K.

Roller Skating Rules for Outdoor Skating
(conventional and in-line skates)

- Give pedestrians the right-of-way.
- Obey all laws about skating on the sidewalks or in the street.
- Don't race out of alleys and driveways.
- Avoid skating on chipped, broken, or rough surfaces. Watch out for rocks, branches, and trees.

- Don't skate on other people's property without their permission.
- Come to a complete stop and look in all directions for traffic before crossing streets.
- Obey traffic laws, signs, and signals.
- Don't skate in the street in traffic.
- Avoid uncontrolled coasting and skating down inclines.
- Don't hitch onto bicycles, cars, or trucks.
- Don't skate outdoors at night.
- Check your equipment before skating. Be sure all fittings are tight.
- Wear the proper protective clothing (wrist guards, helmet, knee and elbow pads).

NOTE for Akela: Ask your son's den leader to show you "Cub Scout Sports: Roller Skating" in the *Cub Scout Academics and Sports Program Guide*.

HIGH JUMP

There are two styles of high jumping. In one, the jumper approaches the bar from the side, swings the leg nearest the bar up and over, and follows with the other leg in a scissors kick.

In the other style, the jumper rolls over the bar by leaping and turning the whole body toward the bar. While going over, the jumper is looking down at the bar.

SPRINT START

Because sprints are short races, a sprinter must get a fast start and run at full speed all the way.

To make a fast start, a sprinter crouches low and leans forward, with all fingers of both hands touching the ground at the starting line. One foot is far behind the other, with the heels off the ground. At the signal, the sprinter shoves off hard with the rear foot and is at full stride right away.

LONG JUMP

In the standing long jump, the jumper leaps as far as he can from the starting line into a sandpit. In the running long jump, the jumper is allowed to run up to the line before leaping.

Both standing and running long jumpers try to fall forward rather than backward when they land.

21 Sales

The idea of selling something goes back a long way. People were trading things even before money was invented. When people traded, they would give something for something else they wanted more. In a sale, both parties should feel that they're better off than they were before the sale. Money is an easier way of keeping track of how much things are worth.

NOTE for Akela: For safety reasons, all sales must be under the direct supervision of a parent, guardian, or other trusted adult.

Requirements

___a. Take part in a council- or pack-sponsored money-earning sales program. Keep track of the sales you make yourself. When the program is over, add up the sales that you have made.

___b. Help with a garage sale or rummage sale. This can be with your family or a neighbor, or it can be a church, school, or pack event.

NO.	DATE	AKELA'S OK	✓ DEN CHART
21.			
21.			

Before you sell something, check with your local council to get permission to wear your Cub Scout uniform. People should buy your product because they want it, not because you are a Cub Scout. Take pride in your appearance; remember, you are representing the entire Scouting organization.

Collecting Things

Many people like to collect things as a hobby. Some things that are collected are stamps, coins, and emblems. Collections are just for fun, but you can't help but learn something about other places when you find a stamp, coin, or emblem from somewhere a long way from where you live.

Requirements

___a. Start a stamp collection. You can get information about stamp collecting at any U.S. post office.

___b. Mount and display a collection of emblems, coins, or other items to show at a pack meeting. This can be any kind of collection. Every time you show a different kind of collection, it counts as one requirement.

___c. Start your own library. Keep your own books and pamphlets in order by subject. List the title, author, and subject of each on an index card and keep the cards in a file box, or use a computer program to store the information.

No.	Date	Akela's OK	✓ Den Chart
22.			
22.			
22.			
22.			

STAMP COLLECTIONS

Boys' Life magazine has many ads for stamps and other things that can be collected. If an ad says that stamps will be sent "on approval," it means that you will have to pay for the stamps sent to you or mail them back. Some companies will give free stamps if you agree to let them send you others "on approval." You should not order these stamps unless you have enough money to buy them or pay for the postage to mail them back.

DISPLAYING A COLLECTION

23   Maps

When explorers scout a new land, they make maps to show others what they find. Maps mean adventure, excitement, and imaginary trips. They are also useful for exploring your town and state.

NOTE for Akela: Ask your son's den leader to show you "Cub Scout Academics: Geography" in the *Cub Scout Academics and Sports Program Guide.*

Requirements

___a. Look up your state on a U.S. map. What other states touch its borders?

___b. Find your city or town on a map of your state. How far do you live from the state capital?

___c. In which time zone do you live? How many time zones are there in the United States?

___d. Make a map showing the route from your home to your school or den meeting place.

___e. Mark a map showing the way to a place you would like to visit that is at least 50 miles from your home.

NO.	DATE	AKELA'S OK	✓ DEN CHART
23.			
23.			
23.			
23.			
23.			

ALASKA
12:00

PACIFIC
1:00

MOUNTAIN
2:00

CENTRAL
3:00

EASTERN
4:00

HAWAII-
ALEUTIAN
11:00

STATES	CAPITALS
ALABAMA	MONTGOMERY
ALASKA	JUNEAU
ARIZONA	PHOENIX
ARKANSAS	LITTLE ROCK
CALIFORNIA	SACRAMENTO
COLORADO	DENVER
CONNECTICUT	HARTFORD
DELAWARE	DOVER
FLORIDA	TALLAHASSEE
GEORGIA	ATLANTA
HAWAII	HONOLULU
IDAHO	BOISE
ILLINOIS	SPRINGFIELD
INDIANA	INDIANAPOLIS
IOWA	DES MOINES
KANSAS	TOPEKA
KENTUCKY	FRANKFORT
LOUISIANA	BATON ROUGE
MAINE	AUGUSTA
MARYLAND	ANNAPOLIS
MASSACHUSETTS	BOSTON
MICHIGAN	LANSING
MINNESOTA	ST. PAUL
MISSISSIPPI	JACKSON
MISSOURI	JEFFERSON CITY
MONTANA	HELENA
NEBRASKA	LINCOLN
NEVADA	CARSON CITY
NEW HAMPSHIRE	CONCORD
NEW JERSEY	TRENTON
NEW MEXICO	SANTE FE
NEW YORK	ALBANY
NORTH CAROLINA	RALEIGH
NORTH DAKOTA	BISMARCK
OHIO	COLUMBUS
OKLAHOMA	OKLAHOMA CITY
OREGON	SALEM
PENNSYLVANIA	HARRISBURG
RHODE ISLAND	PROVIDENCE
SOUTH CAROLINA	COLUMBIA
SOUTH DAKOTA	PIERRE
TENNESSEE	NASHVILLE
TEXAS	AUSTIN
UTAH	SALT LAKE CITY
VERMONT	MONTPELIER
VIRGINIA	RICHMOND
WASHINGTON	OLYMPIA
WEST VIRGINIA	CHARLESTON
WISCONSIN	MADISON
WYOMING	CHEYENNE

American Indian Life

There were people living all over what is now called North and South America when Christopher Columbus arrived here. He called the people he met "Indians" because he thought he was in the East Indies. That name stuck, and today many call themselves "American Indians."

American peoples have made many contributions to humanity. The three sister plants—corn, beans, and squash—are examples. Another example is that the people who are often called "Iroquois" shared the wisdom of their government; some parts of their Great Law of Peace are in the United States Constitution.

Requirements

___a. American Indian people live in every part of what is now the continental United States. Find the name of the American Indian nation that lives or has lived where you live now. Learn about these people.

___b. Learn, make equipment for, and play two American Indian or other native American games with members of your den. Be able to tell the rules, who won, and what the score was.

___c. Learn what the American Indian people in your area (or another area) used for shelter before contact with the Europeans. Learn what American Indian people in that area used for shelter today. Make a model of one of these shelters, historic or modern. Compare the kind of shelter you made with the others made in your den.

No.	Date	Akela's OK	✓ Den Chart
24.			
24.			
24.			

AMERICAN INDIAN GAMES

Some American Indian games help make future hunters, trackers, and caregivers as players learn to be quick of hand and sharp of eye. Others teach us that not everything is ours to keep—it may be here today and gone tomorrow. Try your hand at these.

MOTOWU. This is a game played by the Hopi Indians in Arizona. It's played with feathered darts made from corncobs. When you have corn on the cob, save the cobs and dry them. Cut them all to the same length, about 3½ to 4 inches, and smooth them with a piece of coarse sandpaper glued to a wood block. Make holes at both ends. Using white glue, glue a 2½-inch stick or dowel in the smaller end and two turkey feathers in the big end. You will need at least four darts.

MOTOWU

Place two flower pots or baskets about 10 inches in diameter 12 to 15 feet apart. In turn, each player throws two darts at the same time. The darts are held in one hand with the index finger between them. You can throw directly at the basket or toss them up in the air, which makes them spin. Both darts must go into the basket; the first player to get two darts in at the same time wins the game.

POKEAN. Residents of Zuni Pueblo in New Mexico play this game. They make a kind of shuttlecock from corn husks and feathers. Save the husks from corn and dry them, but don't let them get so dry that they are brittle. Make your pokean while the husks are still soft enough to bend. You will need three corn husks 1½ inches wide and 6 or 7 inches long, and a fourth husk about ¾ inch wide and 5 inches long. Take one of the three large husks and fold it in thirds to make a pad. Lay the other two big husks on a flat surface to form a cross. Put the pad in the center of the cross. Fold the bottom husk over the top husk and the pad. Fold the top husk up and bring the ends together at the top over the center. Don't twist. Wrap the ends with the small husk. Wrap a string snugly two or three times around the ends and tie. Glue three craft feathers into the top with white glue. They will make the pokean twirl in the air.

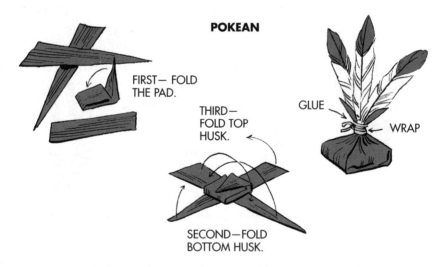

POKEAN

FIRST— FOLD THE PAD.

THIRD— FOLD TOP HUSK.

GLUE

WRAP

SECOND—FOLD BOTTOM HUSK.

Each player tries to keep his pokean in the air by hitting it with his hand. The object of the game is to count the number of times you can hit the pokean to keep it in the air before it falls. The player with the highest score wins the game.

AMERICAN INDIAN HOUSES. In the old days, American Indian peoples used materials found in their environments to build their homes. Those who lived on the Great Plains built tepees, cone-shaped shelters covered with hides (often buffalo). Today, Plains peoples often make tepees covered with canvas, as many tents are covered. Some nations in the southwest built stone houses under overhanging cliffs (cliff dwellings). The Navajo people used short logs, bark, and earth to build round-shaped houses called *hogans*. Some Navajo people continue to live in hogans. In the far north, many peoples built houses of snow blocks.

Today most American Indians live in condos, apartments, trailers, and houses just as non-Indians do; some use their traditional shelters for ceremonies or camping.

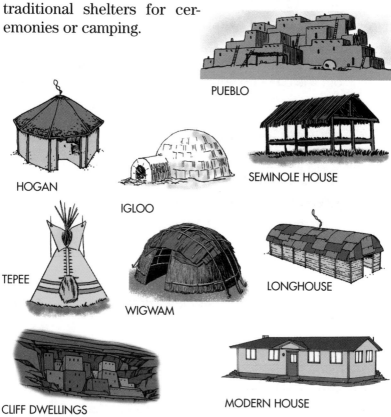

PUEBLO

HOGAN

IGLOO

SEMINOLE HOUSE

TEPEE

WIGWAM

LONGHOUSE

CLIFF DWELLINGS

MODERN HOUSE

Requirements

___a. Learn about the ten essential items you need for a hike or campout. Assemble your own kit of essential items. Explain why each item is "essential."

___b. Go on a short hike with your den, following the buddy system. Explain how the buddy system works and why it is important to you to follow it. Tell what to do if you are lost.

___c. Participate with your den in front of the pack at a campfire.

___d. Participate with your pack on an overnight campout. Help put up your tent and help set up the campsite.

___e. Participate with your den in a religious service during an overnight campout or other Cub Scouting event.

___f. Attend day camp in your area.

___g. Attend resident camp in your area.

___h. Earn the Cub Scout Leave No Trace Award (see page 283).

No.	Date	Akela's OK	✓ Den Chart
25.			
25.			
25.			
25.			

25.			
25.			
25.			
25.			

OUTDOOR ESSENTIALS

1. First aid kit
2. Filled water bottle
3. Flashlight
4. Trail food
5. Sunscreen
6. Whistle
7. Map and compass
8. Rain gear
9. Pocket knife
10. Matches or fire starters

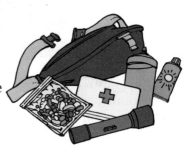

Is there anything else you think should be in the kit? Write it here_____

_____

THE BUDDY SYSTEM

- Everyone has a buddy.
- Your buddy goes everywhere with you, and you go everywhere with him.
- Know where your buddy is at all times.

If you think you are lost, stop!

S— Sit down in the open (don't move or hide). Stay where you are so rescuers can find you. Don't try to find your way back!

T— Think. Be calm; help will come.

O— Observe. Look around. Make yourself "big" (hang up bright clothes, make a rock arrow that points to you, etc.). Blow your whistle three times if you hear rescuers.

P— Plan. Keep dry, curl up to keep warm, drink lots of water.

The buddy system is important. If you get hurt or lost, your buddy will be able to help you. Two people can often solve a problem better than one.

CAMPFIRES ARE A SPECIAL TIME TO HAVE FUN!

- Sing a fun song that everyone knows. Or teach everyone a simple new song.
- Present a short skit. Make sure that everyone can hear you.
- Tell a joke. It's okay if they have heard it before.

We camped at: _____

My favorite part was: _____

_____

Getting set to be a
Webelos Scout

When you have completed the third grade (or are 10 years old), you can join a Webelos den and wear the Webelos uniform.

You can earn 20 activity badges. Do you like science? You can earn the activity badges for Geologist, Scientist, and Naturalist.

Perhaps you like the outdoor life. Well, you'll find activity badges for Outdoorsman, Sportsman, Athlete, Forester, and Aquanaut.

AQUANAUT

ATHLETE

FORESTER

GEOLOGIST

NATURALIST

OUTDOORSMAN

SCIENTIST

SPORTSMAN

There's much more. As a Webelos Scout, you also can earn the Artist, Citizen, Communicator, Craftsman, Engineer, Family Member, Fitness, Handyman, Readyman, Scholar, Showman, and Traveler activity badges.

ARTIST	CITIZEN	COMMUNICATOR	CRAFTSMAN
ENGINEER	FAMILY MEMBER	FITNESS	HANDYMAN
READYMAN	SCHOLAR	SHOWMAN	TRAVELER

There are two reasons for all these activities. One is to offer you more fun. The other is to prepare you to be a Boy Scout. As a matter of fact, you will have the option of wearing the tan/olive uniform when you become a Webelos Scout.

To be a Boy Scout, you must have completed the fifth grade **and** be at least 10 years old or be age 11 or have earned the Arrow of Light Award and be at least 10 years old. You'll be ready to do that if you join the Webelos den and take part in the activities.

Some packs hold a special ceremony at the pack meeting to welcome new Webelos Scouts into the Webelos den.

How to Wear Cub Scout Insignia

DIRECTIONS FOR PLACEMENT

The diagrams on the inside back cover of this book will show you the shapes and locations of the insignia a Cub Scout can be eligible to wear.

SLEEVE INSIGNIA

All Cub Scouts, regardless of rank, wear the sleeve insignia indicated. Remove old insignia before attaching new.

POCKET INSIGNIA

When a Cub Scout earns the Bear badge, he wears it centered on the left side of the left pocket. When he earns a Gold Arrow Point, it goes ¾-inch below the Bear badge. Silver Arrow Points go directly below the Gold in two rows. The size of a Cub Scout's shirt pocket depends on his shirt size, but you will find that his Tiger Cub, Bobcat, Wolf, and Bear badges will fit easily on the average-size pocket. The Progress Toward Ranks is worn on the right pocket.

TO SEW

Use a fine overhand, back, blind, or buttonhole stitch to sew on the insignia. The thread should match the border of the emblem. When using a sewing machine, follow the manufacturer's instructions for stitching badges and emblems.

Cub Scout World Conservation Award

The Cub Scout World Conservation Award is an international award that Bear Cub Scouts can earn by doing the following things:

___ Complete Achievement 5.

___ Complete all requirements in two of the following three electives:

    ___ 2. Weather

    ___ 12. Nature Crafts

    ___ 15. Water and Soil Conservation

___ Participate in a den or pack conservation project in addition to the above.

After you have done all of these things, ask your den leader to order your award.

This award can be earned only once while you are a Cub Scout.

Approved _____
                                 Akela

Cub Scout Leave No Trace Awareness Award

Leave No Trace is a plan that helps you to be more concerned about your environment. It also helps you protect it for future generations.

You can earn the Cub Scout Leave No Trace Awareness Award by doing the following things:

Cub Scout Leave No Trace Pledge

I promise to practice the Leave No Trace frontcountry guidelines wherever I go:

1. Plan ahead.
2. Stick to trails.
3. Manage your pet.
4. Leave what you find.
5. Respect other visitors.
6. Trash your trash.

_____
Signature

1. Discuss with your leader or parent/guardian the importance of the Leave No Trace frontcountry guidelines.
2. On three separate outings, practice the frontcountry guidelines of Leave No Trace.
3. Complete Achievement 12, "Family Outdoor Adventures."
4. Participate in a Leave No Trace–related service project.
5. Promise to practice the Leave No Trace frontcountry guidelines by signing the Cub Scout Leave No Trace Pledge.
6. Draw a poster to illustrate the Leave No Trace frontcountry guidelines and display it at a pack meeting.

After you have done these things, ask your den leader to order your award.

Approved _____
Akela

NOTE for Akela: Ask your den leader for more information on the Leave No Trace frontcountry guidelines and this award.

Cub Scout
Outdoor Activity Award

Tiger Cubs, Wolf and Bear Cub Scouts, and Webelos Scouts have the opportunity to earn the Cub Scout Outdoor Activity Award. Boys may earn the award in each of the program years as long as the requirements are completed each year. The first time the award is earned, the boy will receive the pocket flap award, which is to be worn on the right pocket flap of the uniform shirt. Each successive time the award is earned, a wolf track pin may be added to the flap. Leaders should encourage boys to build on skills and experiences from previous years when working on the award for a successive year.

Requirements

ALL RANKS
Attend Cub Scout day camp or Cub Scout/Webelos Scout resident camp. (To be completed after September 1, 2004. Award was launched in late August 2004.)

RANK-SPECIFIC
Tiger Cubs. Complete one requirement in Achievement 5, "Let's Go Outdoors" *(Tiger Cub Handbook)* and complete three of the outdoor activities listed below.

Wolf Cub Scouts. Assemble the "Six Essentials for Going Outdoors" *(Wolf Handbook,* Elective 23b) and discuss their purpose, and complete four of the outdoor activities listed below.

Bear Cub Scouts. Earn the Cub Scout Leave No Trace Award *(Bear Handbook,* Elective 25h) and compete five of the outdoor activities listed below.

Webelos Scouts. Earn the Outdoorsman Activity Badge *(Webelos Handbook);* and complete six of the outdoor activities listed below.

OUTDOOR ACTIVITIES

With your den, pack, or family:

1. Participate in a nature hike in your local area. This can be on an organized, marked trail, or just a hike to observe nature in your area.

2. Participate in an outdoor activity such as a picnic or park fun day.

3. Explain the buddy system and tell what to do if lost. Explain the importance of cooperation.

4. Attend a pack overnighter. Be responsible by being prepared for the event.

5. Complete an outdoor service project in your community.

6. Complete a nature/conservation project in your area. This project should involve improving, beautifying, or supporting natural habitats. Discuss how this project helped you to respect nature.

7. Earn the Summertime Pack Award.

8. Participate in a nature observation activity. Describe or illustrate and display your observations at a den or pack meeting.

9. Participate in an outdoor aquatic activity. This can be an organized swim meet or just a den or pack swim.

10. Participate in an outdoor campfire program. Perform in a skit, sing a song, or take part in a ceremony.

11. Participate in an outdoor sporting event.

12. Participate in an outdoor Scout's Own or other worship service.

13. Explore a local city, county, state, or national park. Discuss with your den how a good citizen obeys the park rules.

After you have done these things, ask your den leader to order your award.

Approved _____
Akela

Cub Scout
Academics and Sports

You can have fun and learn new skills when you take part in the Cub Scout Academics and Sports program. Just by learning about and participating in an academic subject or sport, you can earn belt loops and pins.

Each academic and sport subject is included in the *Cub Scout Academics and Sports Program Guide*, which tells you what the requirements are for earning the special recognition of belt loops and pins.

You can take part in the program at home, in your den or pack, or in activities in your community. Archery and BB-gun shooting are restricted to day camps, Cub Scout/ Webelos Scout resident camps, council-managed family camping programs, or to council activities where there are properly trained supervisors and all standards for BSA shooting sports are enforced. Ask your den leader to tell you more about the Cub Scout Academics and Sports program and the many academics and sports subjects that you can explore!

| Art | Astronomy | Badminton | Baseball |

| Basketball | Bicycling | Bowling | Chess |

| Citizenship | Collecting | Communicating | Computers |

Fishing

Flag Football

Geography

Geology

Golf

Gymnastics

Heritages

Ice Skating

Language and Culture

Map and Compass

Marbles

Mathematics

Music

Physical Fitness

Roller Skating

Science

Snow Ski and Board Sports

Soccer

Softball

Swimming

Table Tennis

Tennis

Ultimate

Volleyball

Weather

Wildlife Conservation

Bear Trail Record

To earn your Bear badge, you must complete twelve achievements. You must earn one for God (either achievement 1 or 2), three for Country (from achievements 3, 4, 5, 6, and 7), four for Family (from achievements 8, 9, 10, 11, 12, and 13), and four for Self (from achievements 14, 15, 16, 17, 18, 19, 20, 21, 22, 23, and 24).

Most achievements have several requirements. When you complete a requirement, draw a circle around the letter for that requirement on this page. When you have done enough requirements to complete the achievement, put an "X" in the box by the achievement.

Achievements that were not used to earn the Bear badge may be used as electives. However, note that unused parts of achievements that were used for the Bear badge may **not** be counted toward Arrow Points. Mark the letter for that requirement with an "X."

On the next page, keep a list of all of your elective credits. You earn an Arrow Point for every ten elective credits you complete.

	Do ▼	**of these** ▼
Do one for GOD		
❏ 1. Ways We Worship	2	(a) (b)
❏ 2. Emblems of Faith	1	(a)
Do three for COUNTRY		(a) (b) (c) (d) (e) (f) (g)
❏ 3. What Makes America Special?	a and j + 2	(h) (i) (j)
❏ 4. Tall Tales	all 3	(a) (b) (c)
❏ 5. Sharing Your World with Wildlife	any 4	(a) (b) (c) (d) (e)
❏ 6. Take Care of Your Planet	any 3	(a) (b) (c) (d) (e) (f) (g)
❏ 7. Law Enforcement Is a Big Job	all 6	(a) (b) (c) (d) (e) (f)